Moving from comfortable prayers to bold and faith-filled prayers doesn't happen automatically. I love how Craig teaches us, urges us onward, and models how to have the kind of prayer life we've always wanted. It's not about always getting what we want. It's about growing closer to the heart of God and truly trusting him with whatever happens next.

—Lysa TerKeurst, *New York Times* bestselling
author; president, Proverbs 31 Ministries

The Christian life was never meant to be a safe life. Yet all too often we settle for comfort over risk and abandon our purpose in the process. Pastor Craig challenges us to put it all on the line with God and build our faith for a life of risk as we walk in our God-given purpose.

—Christine Caine, bestselling author;
founder, A21 and Propel Women

In this book, you'll feel yourself neither pushed nor pulled toward more prayers that feel like they merely bounce off of the ceiling. Instead, you're invited to pray the kind of dangerous prayers which have the power to change yourself, the people you love, and the people God loves—which is everybody.

—Bob Goff, author, *New York Times* bestsellers
Love Does and *Everybody Always*

To lean in to prayer the way Pastor Craig so brilliantly expounds on is to lean in to prayers that will change the world, and just might change you at the same time. This book is profound and prophetic and so, so helpful.

—Jefferson Bethke, author, *New York
Times* bestselling *Jesus > Religion*

This book will challenge you to trade your stale, safe prayer life for one brimming with danger and excitement. Discover how to offer genuine and gutsy prayers, the kind of dangerous prayers that change not only hearts but also our world.

—Lisa Bevere, *New York Times* bestselling
author, *Without Rival* and *Girls with Swords*

If your prayer life needs a boost, you will enjoy this powerful new book. It will build your faith, strengthen your walk with God, and teach you to pray in dangerous ways.

—Mark Batterson, *New York Times* bestselling author,
The Circle Maker; lead pastor, National Community Church

Craig Groeschel is convinced our prayers need to get bigger. In *Dangerous Prayers,* he tells us why and how. Taken to heart, this book has the potential to radically transform not only how you pray but also how you view the world and how you view God's activity in the world. Thank you, Craig!

—Andy Stanley, author; communicator;
founder, North Point Ministries

If there's one mistake in prayer we should avoid at all costs, it's playing it too safe. In *Dangerous Prayers,* my pastor and friend, Craig Groeschel, will challenge you to embrace the uncertainty and lean into a more daring, more fulfilling prayer life.

—Steven Furtick, pastor, Elevation Church;
New York Times bestselling author

This isn't another sweet book about the practice of prayer that will leave you feeling condemned and ashamed that you don't pray more. On the contrary, it's about what happens when we sincerely talk with a living God. And *that* can be beautifully, wonderfully dangerous.

—Judah Smith, lead pastor, Churchome

DANGEROUS
PRAYERS

Also by Craig Groeschel

DANGEROUS PRAYERS

BECAUSE FOLLOWING JESUS
WAS NEVER MEANT TO BE SAFE

CRAIG GROESCHEL

ZONDERVAN®

ZONDERVAN

Dangerous Prayers
Copyright © 2020 by Craig Groeschel

Requests for information should be addressed to:
Zondervan, *3900 Sparks Dr. SE, Grand Rapids, Michigan 49546*

Zondervan titles may be purchased in bulk for educational, business, fundraising, or promotional use. For information, please email SpecialMarkets@Zondervan.com.

ISBN 978-0-310-34312-7 (hardcover)

ISBN 978-0-310-35814-5 (international trade paper edition)

ISBN 978-0-310-35595-3 (audio)

ISBN 978-0-310-34313-4 (ebook)

Craig Groeschel is represented by Thomas J. Winters of Winters & King, Inc., Tulsa, Oklahoma.

Cover design: Stephen Cox
Cover illustration: Public Domain Illustration
Back cover photo: Robby Doland
Interior design: Denise Froehlich

Printed in the United States of America

19 20 21 22 23 LSC 10 9 8 7 6 5 4 3 2 1

This book is dedicated to my mom.
Thank you for praying faithfully all those years.
Your prayers made all the difference.
I love you and honor you.

Thank you for purchasing
Dangerous Prayers!
All of the author's proceeds
from this book will support
Bible access and translation
efforts through the
YouVersion Bible App.

CONTENTS

PART 3: SEND ME

WHY YOUR PRAYERS NEED TO BE DANGEROUS

H ey, Craig, do you believe God still does miracles?"

"Of course," I said.

"Good—because your prayers are so *lame*."

I tried to laugh with him, but my friend's joke stung—mostly because he was right. We had just left a prayer service together, back when I started working in ministry. My buddy knew me well enough to tease me, but I suspect he was also making a point. Left speechless, I offered no defense as I processed the truth of his observation. I couldn't deny that he voiced a secret I already knew but didn't want to admit: my prayers were pathetic.

As a young pastor at the time, I should have had a handle on prayer. It's one of those job responsibilities, like preaching and greeting people after the service, I should've mastered.

But praying long, focused, eloquent, and powerful prayers to the God-I-couldn't-see had always been challenging for me. I wasn't comfortable praying in a King James dialect of *thees* and *thous*—like trying to perform Shakespeare. But I wasn't satisfied just rambling in a shoot-the-breeze, best-buddy tone with the Creator and Sustainer of the universe either.

And even when I did pray, I had a difficult time focusing for long. Which meant I'd try even harder the next time. But no matter how hard I'd try, I always seemed to fall back into the same old prayer rut. I'd pray about the same things. In the same ways. Usually around the same time.

Looking back, I wonder if sometimes God got bored with my prayers. When I'd pray, "Lord, show us traveling mercies and keep us safe," I could imagine him saying, "What are you worried about? Just drive the speed limit and wear your seatbelt. You'll be fine." Or when I prayed, "God, bless our food," I just knew he was probably thinking, "Really? You want me to bless boxed macaroni and cheese and some potato chips?"

As I studied the Bible more, I marveled at the variety of prayers spoken by God's people. Not only did they pray about things that were incredibly personal—to conceive a child, for instance (1 Sam. 1:27)—but also their prayers were often so practical, for food and provision (Matt. 6:11) and escape from their enemies (Ps. 59:1–2). Sometimes they seemed to gently whisper to a loving God. Other times they yelled at him in agony and frustration.

They often pleaded with God sincerely. Then later they'd

cry out from the depths of their anguish and rail at God like a tired toddler thrashing in the arms of a parent. They prayed for boldness to share their faith. They prayed for walls, both internally and externally, to fall. Daniel prayed for the mouths of hungry lions to be shut, and Jonah prayed for the belly of a hungry whale to be opened. Gideon prayed for his fleece to be wet one day and dry another. God's people prayed whether they were giddy with joy or crushed by sorrow.

Their prayers were honest. Desperate. Fiery. Gutsy. Real.

And there I was praying that God would keep me safe and bless my burger and fries.

My friend was right.

My prayers were lame.

Maybe you can relate. It's not that you don't believe in prayer. You do. But you're stuck in a rut. You pray about the same struggles and the same requests. In the same way. At the same time. If you even try to pray at all. Like me, you probably know you should pray more. And with more passion. More faith. You want to talk to God and to listen to him, to share an intimate conversation like you would with your spouse or best friend. You really want to but aren't sure how. So your prayers remain safe.

Flat. Dull. Predictable. Stale.

Boring.

My friend's wake-up call convinced me that it was time for a change in my prayer life. For too long, I had tolerated lackluster, faithless, and mostly empty prayers. I knew God wanted more for me, and I wanted to know him more intimately, despite my hesitation about what it would require of me.

To get there, I began by unpacking some of my spiritual baggage. For years, I'd felt deep shame about my half-hearted prayer life—me, a pastor. If you've ever felt insecure about your prayer life, think about what it's like to be a pastor. I'm supposed be a prayer warrior—full of fierce, unrelenting faith and unbridled, Spirit-led power. And yet I found myself drifting while trying to pray.

In the middle of a prayer, whether praying silently or aloud, my mind would bounce from one thing to the next. *Dear God in heaven, I pray that you heal my friend who has cancer. Work in her life now in the name of . . . I really need to go to the hospital to see her again. Oh wait, I haven't changed the oil in the car. And we're out of cereal. The kids are gonna kill me. And Amy has a doctor's appointment today—did we pay that last insurance bill? I can't believe how much it's going up this year! Oh, yeah, this week's sermon—still need to find a strong illustration . . . Oh, I'm sorry, Lord, what were we talking about?*

To make matters even worse, I always dreaded prayer meetings. (Talk about feeling guilty.) They seem to last forever with people who not only know how to pray but also love to pray. Not to mention that whenever you have to hold hands with others in a prayer time, it seems to get weird really quick. On one side is always the Vise. The louder she prays, the harder she squeezes. "God, we bind up the work of the devil, IN JESUS' NAME!" Squeeze. Squeeze. *Squeeze.* Your knuckles turn white as you lose feeling up to your elbow. But then on the other side, you often have the Fish, a cold, pulseless hand barely grasping yours. The Vise cuts off your circulation while the Fish makes you eager to shrug off that clammy appendage passing as a hand.

And there's always the Power Pray-er, the person who loves to pray loud and proud. You know, the one who quotes tons of Bible verses and makes you feel even more inadequate. "God, you said in your Word in Deuteronomy 28 that we would be the head and not the tail. We know from John 3:16, Lord, that you so loved the world." With so many numbers thrown around, by the end you feel like you've been listening to a lecture on accounting.

Then there's always the Competitor. When I was a new Christian in college, I frequently experienced this kind of prayer one-upmanship with my roommate. He'd pray loud and long, sounding so sure of himself, and display his vast knowledge of God and the Bible. Feeling pressure not to be outdone, I'd up my game but usually found myself taking it too far. Since I didn't know much about the Bible then, I'd just roll out things that sounded powerful and Bible-like. "God, you said in your Word that you are not only Jehovah Jireh but that you are also Jehovah, um, let's see, um, Jehovah Ni . . . um, *Nissan*. Yes—you are Jehovah NISSAN! And, Lord, you are good. You are good to, um, to the . . . God, you are good to the last drop. And your Word is so sweet, like honey on our lips, and it tastes so good . . . it, um, it melts . . . in our mouths . . .

and not in our hands. Oh, God, like a good neighbor . . . you're always there!"

These weren't my only prayer problems. Too often, praying just didn't make any sense. It seemed like God would often respond quickly to my meaningless requests, like the time I almost jokingly asked God to heal our broken air-conditioning unit, and he did. Then I'd fast for days and pray my guts out for months that God would heal a friend from a disease, and he didn't. Sometimes I believed in the power of prayer, and other times I wondered whether it was all a big waste of time.

Since those early years, I've learned quite a bit about prayer. For one thing, God hates showy prayers, so there's no pressure, no right way other than being open and honest with him. Jesus repeatedly railed against the Pharisees for praying long, loud, and fancy prayers that lacked authenticity. Christ taught us, "And when you pray, do not be like the hypocrites, for they love to pray standing in the synagogues and on the street corners to be seen by others. Truly I tell you, they have received their reward in full" (Matt. 6:5).

> God hates showy prayers, so there's no pressure, no right way other than being open and honest with him.

Instead of long, loud, and fancy, the prayers that move God are simple, authentic, and heartfelt. But simple is not the same as safe. And that's the reason I'm compelled to write this book. The biggest mistake I made in my prayer life, the reason my prayers were so lame, is because I prayed too safely. I was in a comfort zone with God, built on lame, half-hearted communication. I wasn't on fire and I wasn't cold. My prayers were tepid. But safe, lukewarm prayers don't draw us closer to God or help us reveal his love to this world.

Prayers are inherently dangerous.

This idea about prayer dawned on me while reading about Jesus talking to his Father in the garden of Gethsemane, just a short time before he gave his life on the cross. Knowing what was ahead, Jesus asked God if there was any other way. Then Jesus, not just a regular disciple or a person in the Bible, but J-E-S-U-S, the Son of God, prayed a vulnerable and dangerous prayer of submission: "Yet I want your will to be done, not mine" (Luke 22:42 NLT).

Jesus never asks us to do something he wouldn't do himself. He calls us to a life of faith, not a life of comfort. Instead of coming to him for a safer, easier, stress-free lifestyle, the Son of God challenges us to risk loving others more than ourselves. Instead of indulging our daily desires, he calls us to deny them for something eternal. Instead of living by what we want, he tells us to pick up our crosses daily and follow his example. In this book, we'll dig more deeply into these ideas through three powerful prayers drawn from Scripture. These three prayers may be short. They may be simple. They may be straightforward. But they are not safe.

In the next three sections of this book, we'll attempt to stretch our faith, expand our hearts, and open our lives to God praying these three dangerous prayers:

SEARCH ME.

BREAK ME.

SEND ME.

When we're seeking to communicate with God in real, vulnerable, and intimate prayer, he's not wrapping us in a bubble of spiritual safety. Instead he bursts our what's-in-it-for-me bubble and invites us to trust him when we don't know what he will do next. Some days we feel blessed. Other days we face challenges, opposition, and persecution. But every moment of dangerous prayer will be filled with his presence.

I worry that for a lot of people prayer is like buying a lottery ticket, a chance at a life here on earth that's problem free, stress free, pain free. For others, prayer is merely a sentimental routine, like reciting favorite song lyrics or a beloved nursery rhyme from childhood. Yet others pray only because they feel even guiltier if they don't.

But none of these prayers reflect the life Jesus came to give us.

Instead, he called us to leave everything to follow him.

When a rich and powerful young man approached Jesus to ask some weighty spiritual questions, Jesus didn't lower the bar in his response. Instead, "Jesus looked at him and loved him. 'One thing you lack,' he said. 'Go, sell everything you have and give to the poor, and you will have treasure in heaven. Then come, follow me'" (Mark 10:21).

I've always been moved by the fact that *before* Jesus asked this man to leave everything, Jesus made this bold request in love. Jesus wanted the best for this man, who had everything on the outside but still lived with a void on the inside. Jesus loved him and almost dared him to abandon it all to follow him.

Jesus didn't just challenge others to leave their own wills behind. He too lived a dangerous faith. He touched lepers. Showed grace to prostitutes. And stood bravely in the face of danger. Then he told us we could do what he did—and more.

And that's why we can't settle for simply asking God to bless our food or "be with us today."

Are you ready for more? Are you sick of playing it safe? Are you ready to pray daring, faith-filled, God-honoring, life-changing, world-transforming prayers?

If you are, then this book is for you.

But be warned. There will be bumps. When you start to pray things like "search me, break me, send me," you may experience valleys. Attacks. Trials. Pain. Hardship. Discouragement. Even heartbreak. But there will also be the joy of faith, the marvel of miracles, the relief of surrender, and the pleasure of pleasing God.

It's time to stop praying safe.

It's time to start talking, really talking—and really listening—to God.

It's time for dangerous prayers.

PART 1

SEARCH ME

Search me, God, and know my heart; test me and know my anxious thoughts. See if there is any offensive way in me, and lead me in the way everlasting.

—PSALM 139:23–24

SEARCH ME

One of my first breakthroughs about prayer occurred years ago when my mother had surgery. My family and I had gathered in Mom's hospital room, trying to reassure her that the procedure would go smoothly the next morning. She was understandably nervous, so when a middle-aged man in a black suit and clerical collar knocked and asked if she would like him to pray for her, she exclaimed, "Well, of course I want you to pray for me!"

He smiled and nodded, confident in his demeanor as he produced a small well-worn leather book from his suit pocket. Standing beside her bed, he asked, "What is your denominational preference?"

"I'm just a . . . well . . . just a regular Christian. I don't have a denominational preference. Just Protestant."

I knew she had grown up attending a Lutheran school, but also that our family had been attending a Methodist church for as long as I could remember. It never seemed to be a big deal, really. Apparently, though, the chaplain didn't share our casual attitude about denominations. "Uh, I'm sorry, ma'am," he said, shifting his weight from one leg to the other. "It would just help me know which prayer to read if you could pick a denomination that you're comfortable with."

"Well, let's just go with Methodist then." Mom smiled politely, eager to help the chaplain do his job.

Relieved, he returned her smile and thumbed through his little book until he found the page he wanted. He then began reading the prayer, and honestly, the only way any of us knew it was a prayer was because he told us. With his cheery monotone voice, the chaplain could have been reading a nursery rhyme or his grocery list.

Before he could finish, Mom interrupted him. And you'd have to know my mom to fully grasp the impact of her interruption. She's the nicest, most thoughtful, caring person you will ever meet. She would give you her last dollar, walk across town to help you out, and write you a three-page thank-you note for the gift you sent her. She's absolutely as kind as they come—but she's also known for being a bit ornery. Not only does she enjoy having fun, she rarely minces words. If she thinks it, she will say it. Without holding back.

While the chaplain was still reading from his prescribed Methodist prayer, my mother interrupted. Loud enough to be heard all the way to the nurses' station, she playfully called out, "Will somebody please find me a chaplain who knows how to pray his own prayers?"

At first, we all tried not to laugh, but it was impossible to hold it in. Even the chaplain, poor guy, had to grin. Everyone in my family still chuckles when we retell this story about Mom's frank assessment of this man's prayer. But Mom made a good point.

Praying from the heart is personal and unmistakable.

There's certainly nothing wrong with reading a prayer or using someone else's words to pray. In fact, reading prayers can be a good starting point in learning to pray your own. Over time, though, if you want to know God intimately, you will begin to pray more unscripted prayers that come straight from your heart. As your faith grows, your prayers will likely well up deep inside you. You may not even know how to express them in words. They're simply communication between you and your Father, the living God Almighty. Deeply personal and just as unique as your fingerprint.

> **Praying from the heart is personal and unmistakable.**

You don't have to look far in the Psalms to see the honest cries from the heart of David. He questioned God. He complained to God. He petitioned God. From the depths of his soul, David cried out to his heavenly Father, asking, "How long, LORD? Will you forget me forever? How long will you hide your face from me? How long must I wrestle with my thoughts and day after day have sorrow in my heart? How long will my enemy triumph over me?" (Ps. 13:1–2).

But I'm afraid many of us aren't comfortable praying openly and freely. We assume there's a right way or a better way or a more eloquent way. We tend to stumble into ruts and pray for the same things over and over. We get bored with our prayers.

And if we get bored praying, then I wonder if we're really praying.

TRUTH OR DARE

Prayer is sacred communication, the language of longing, a divine dialogue between you and your heavenly Father, your Abba, your Daddy. When you pray, the God of the universe listens. And not only does he listen, but he also cares. About what you have to say. About all the things you carry around in your heart that no one else knows about. Maybe even some things *you* don't know about. God wants to hear you and speak to you. He wants to communicate with you the same way you sit across from a loved one and enjoy an intimate conversation.

Your prayers matter.

How you pray matters.

What you pray matters.

Your. Prayers. Move. God.

We're told in the Bible that we can "come boldly to the throne of our gracious God" (Heb. 4:16a NLT). We don't have to approach timidly or feel awkward—we can come before him with confidence, assurance, and boldness. When we pray this way, then "we will receive his mercy, and we will find grace to help us when we need it most" (Heb. 4:16b NLT).

Do you need grace in your relationships with other people?

Do you need mercy for all the secret things you struggle with?

Do you need help to get through your day?

I do. In big ways. Every day. And in every way.

So let me share something that's helped me grow some spiritual muscle in place of those wimpy prayers my friend pointed out. They are simply three prayers drawn from the Bible that you can pray and make your own. By this, I simply mean you can pray them in your own words, allowing them to rise up to heaven even as they sink into your bones. They're tools for focusing your prayers and communication with God.

But I must warn you. They're not safe prayers. They're not benign or polite or tepid. You can't just memorize them in hopes of a warm, fuzzy moment with God.

These prayers require faith. Courage. They ask you to risk.

They're almost guaranteed to push you out of your comfort zone. To stretch you. To help you grow righteously uncomfortable. They will require you to look deep within yourself. To stop pretending about certain aspects of your life. To be honest with yourself before the One who knows you better than you know yourself.

These prayers may melt your heart and open an awareness of sin in your life. You may feel compelled to take a bold step of radical faith, trusting God as you follow him and go off script from the predictable pattern of your life. You will likely be challenged to leave spiritual safety, comfort, and convenience behind you.

Instead of a safe, all-about-me prayer, you might pray for others first, hurting for them, hoping for them, reaching out to God on their behalf.

Instead of just asking for protection and safety, you might ask what God wants you to do and where he wants you to go.

Rather than always asking him for more, you might praise him for all the blessings he's already poured into your life. Recognizing all these blessings, you might then reach out to bless someone else.

Instead of just checking a box, your prayers might actually change eternity, shaking hell, scaring demons, and enlarging heaven. Sound extreme? I promise you it's not. More importantly, *God* promises. If you call out to him, God assures you that he hears the cries of your heart.

Your prayers become dangerous.

But following Jesus was never supposed to be safe.

> If you call out to him, God assures you that he hears the cries of your heart.

He promised his followers they would face trouble (see John 16:33). Jesus warned those who faithfully served him that they would be persecuted just like he was (see John 15:20). Jesus alerts us of upcoming challenges. Because we love him, we will face trials and opposition. But even in the middle of painful trials, Jesus invites us to respond with grace and pray what feels like a vulnerable and dangerous prayer. Jesus said, "But I tell you, love your enemies and pray for those who persecute you" (Matt. 5:44). Love those who want to do you harm. And pray for those who are intent on your demise.

Do you dare to pray in a way you've never prayed before? With all of your heart, soul, mind, and the full extent of your being? What would happen in your life and the lives of those around you if you started praying dangerous prayers?

Do you dare to find out?

THE STATE OF YOUR HEART

The first prayer comes from David, and it's a doozy. In the Old Testament we see David squaring off against God's enemies left and right. In a raging fit of jealousy, King Saul falsely accused David of treason and attempting to assassinate the king. Saul sent his full forces after David in repeated attempts to take his life and remove what Saul saw as his biggest threat. And he knew how to hit where it hurts—he claimed David wasn't faithful to his God.

With all his heart, David wanted to please God. He fought against his anger in order to protect and show honor to the king. Yet knowing that his motives weren't always perfect, David surrendered his heart before God and prayed one of the most vulnerable, transparent, and dangerous prayers you'll ever hear. Wanting to honor God in every aspect of his being, David prayed, "Search me, God, and know my heart; test me and know my anxious thoughts. See if there is any offensive way in me, and lead me in the way everlasting" (Ps. 139:23–24).

Not only is this prayer difficult to pray, but it's even more challenging to apply and live out. Because if you have the courage to pray it, then you'll need to exercise the courage to live what God shows you in reply. So don't pray it if you don't mean it.

Be forewarned, this prayer has the potential to convict you. To correct you. To redirect your life. To change the way you see yourself. To change how others see you.

Maybe you're still thinking this is no big deal. Maybe you're wondering why you should ask God to search your heart when he already knows all that's inside you. You know what's in there. He knows what's in there. So why ask something so obvious?

This is where it's tricky. On the surface, it seems like we would know our own hearts. Right? *I know my motives. I know what's most important. I know why I do what I do.* Besides, you might tell yourself, *I've got a good heart. I'm not trying to hurt people. I want to do what's right. My heart is good. I'm praying, aren't I?*

But God's Word actually reveals the exact opposite. It might be a shock when you hear it the first time, but Jeremiah tells us some straight-up truth. Jeremiah was the son of a Levitical priest born around 650 BC. During the reign of King Josiah, God raised up this young prophet to take God's Word to Israel and the nations. Jeremiah flat out says you—along with me and everybody else—don't have a good heart. In fact, not only is your heart not good, but your heart is wicked and sinful in all its ways. The prophet said, "The human heart is the most deceitful of all things, and desperately wicked. Who really knows how bad it is?" (Jer. 17:9 NLT).

It's easy to pretend we are good at heart, but the Bible teaches us that our heart deceives us and is desperately wicked. At its core, our heart is all about self—not Christ. It's about what's temporary—not eternal. It's about what's easy— not what's right. It's obsessed with what we want—not what God wants.

You might think, no, not me. My heart is good. Please remember, without Christ, it's not. If we think it is, we are being deceived by our own heart. Our original nature at birth is sinful. (You never have to teach a two-year-old to be selfish, right?) Our ways are not God's ways. That's why we need Christ. Not just to forgive us, but to transform us. To redirect us. To make us new.

> Our ways are not God's ways. That's why we need Christ. Not just to forgive us, but to transform us. To redirect us. To make us new.

If you still believe you're inherently good, then let me ask you, how often do you lie? If you answer "not that often," then you're probably lying right there. If you answer "never," then I know you're lying.

Research studies reveal that most people tell multiple lies every day. We don't want to hurt someone's feelings. Or we want to make ourselves look good so we exaggerate. But the most common lies are the ones we tell ourselves. Have you ever done this? You tell yourself what you believe is true in your heart: *I won't eat much. I promise. Just a couple of bites.* And the next thing you know you're holding an empty bag of chips or licking the pan clean.

The most common lies are the ones we tell ourselves.

We all rationalize. No one likes to face the ugly truth that they drink too much, that they think about things that they'd be ashamed for anyone else to know, that they laugh at others' mistakes and gossip behind their backs. And the rationalizations continue. You tell yourself, I'm not materialistic; I just like nice things. I'm not a gossip; I'm just telling them so they can pray. I don't have a problem; this is just my one thing I do to cope.

I bet David was tempted to cope when he was running for his life from Saul. He could have used alcohol to escape. He could have turned angry, resentful, and bitter. Or David could have plotted to harm King Saul, justifying his actions in the name of self-preservation. But instead of taking the easy path, David chose a more daring one. The "man after [God's] own heart" (1 Sam. 13:14) decided to pray, knowing that his own heart was capable of tricking him again and again.

Without Christ, your heart is deceitful.

That's why this prayer of David's is crazy dangerous.

"Search my heart, Lord."

HARD CHOICES

I was in high school the first time I came across David's dangerous prayer. On Wednesday nights at our Methodist church, my buddies and I would go to our weekly youth group meeting. While I'm not sure how much I grew spiritually at these meetings, a few things stand out. First would have to be our epic four-square battles. I don't think four square is mentioned in the Bible, but you'd think it was Armageddon considering the way we played it.

I also remember the refreshments in our small cafeteria. Each week, some of the older ladies would bake us goodies—brownies, cookies, lemon bars. Some weeks I went just to see what the spread would be. These Methodist ladies were serious about proving the Bible true when it says, "Taste and see that the LORD is good" (Ps. 34:8).

I also remember our youth pastors didn't last long. Most seemed temporary, like they were just visiting to see if we might be a church they wanted to settle in. It had to be tough, trying to connect with a bunch of moody teenagers all trying to impress each other more than wanting to learn about God. Despite the turnover, one guy had a real impact on me.

I must've been a junior in high school when several of us boarded a small bus to travel to the Methodist campground about two hours from our church. The first day at camp, after a time of worship, our youth pastor taught a lesson on David's introspective prayer asking God to "search him." At the end of his lesson, he encouraged us to go off alone and pray that prayer over and over again, listening for what God might tell us in response. I was into it but had no idea what God was about to set in motion in my life.

I left the crowd and walked to the edge of the playground where the trees hadn't been cut down. The air smelled fresh, like pine, as white clouds unraveled in the blue sky overhead. Sitting near the edge of the tree line, I took the assignment seriously. *It's time I learned to pray—really pray.* I couldn't see anyone else around so I said it out loud: "God, search my heart."

I wish I could tell you that God showed me that my heart was pure, my ways were holy, and my motives all about serving him. But on that day, I distinctly remember sensing an answer to my request. God didn't speak audibly, and I didn't see a sign in the sky. No parting clouds or thunderbolts. I just sensed a very personal and holy presence. And in the same moment that I felt an unmistakable heavenly love, I also simultaneously realized the extent of my sinfulness.

I was such a hypocrite.

My peers had voted me to be president of our youth group, a leader and role model for all the other kids at our church. But my life was a sham as far as my faith was concerned. I acted sincere and serious on Wednesday nights at youth group and then partied with a wilder crowd on the weekend. I pretended like I knew God, but my life and heart revealed how far from him I really was. I put on a show for one crowd and played a completely different role for a more comfortable audience.

So when I paused to pray "Search me" that afternoon at church camp, I was blindsided by the reality of the depths of my sinfulness. Years later I discovered a verse that says it well: "These people come near to me with their mouth and honor me with their lips, but their hearts are far from me" (Isa. 29:13). I gave God lip service, but my heart was wicked. I talked the talk, but I didn't walk the walk. I pretended to be a Christian, but I didn't know the Christ.

It was then that I realized the closer I got to Jesus, the more I'd have to face my shortcomings. My pride. My selfishness. My lust. My critical spirit.

Praying this dangerous prayer that day opened a channel of communication with God I didn't know existed. Instead of simply asking God to do something *for* me, I asked him to reveal something *in* me. And he revealed things to me that day that began my journey toward knowing God personally. It became clear to me that I was a mess. I lied. Cheated. Stole. And did what I wanted no matter who it hurt. What had seemed normal now felt wrong. The life I thought I wanted led me to become someone I hated. Unfortunately, this moment of truth with God didn't change me instantly, but it did help me recognize my spiritual need. I knew that something would need to be different. And I would grow to learn that that *something* was actually learning to love and serve with every fiber of my being a *someone* named Jesus.

Instead of simply asking God to do something *for* you, ask God to reveal something *in* you.

It's a dangerous prayer.

But it's one that could redirect your life.

"Search me, God."

REVEAL MY FEARS

What is it that makes you anxious? Nervous? Unsettled? Afraid?

I'm not talking about normal external fears like snakes, spiders, or the fear of flying. I'm wondering what keeps you up at night, those things that ricochet in your mind and refuse to be quieted. Things like losing your job. Not getting married. Or being stuck in a bad marriage. Having your health fail. Draining your savings account just to get by.

We don't know what exact fears were running through David's mind, but it's clear he was troubled about his safety and perhaps his future. Because after asking God to search his heart, David prayed, "know my anxious thoughts" (Ps. 139:23). He wanted to share his worst fears with God. To face them and give them a name. To trust that God was bigger than any fear David could dream up.

Are you willing to pray such a prayer? "Lord, reveal what

holds my mind hostage. Show me what I fear the most. Go ahead, help me face what terrifies me."

You might wonder why our "anxious thoughts" matter to God. It's not necessarily about our comfort and experiencing a stress-free life. But the answer to this question is perhaps much more important than most of us would understand on the surface.

What we fear matters.

Years ago, I had a revelation about this subject that touched me in a very personal way. God showed me that what I feared the most revealed where I trusted God the least. After the birth of our third daughter, Anna, Amy

What we fear the most often reveals where we trust God the least.

started having physical challenges. At first, we thought it was just fatigue, but when half her body went numb, we feared it was something much worse. Doctor after doctor couldn't provide answers. As her symptoms continued to worsen, my trust in God started to weaken.

This fear led to others, and at night my thoughts snowballed out of control. *What if Amy is dangerously sick? What if I lose her? I won't be able to raise our kids without her. I wouldn't be able to continue to lead the church. I wouldn't want to go on.* Then it hit me. The things that kept me awake at night were the things that I wasn't trusting God to handle. I was holding onto them, ruminating over them, trying to find a way to gain control over them, to solve all my problems, to plan for every contingency. Thankfully, by the grace of God, Amy gradually improved back to full strength, but her challenges exposed one of my worst weaknesses. Fear had consumed me.

What about you? What are the areas that you're clinging to even while allowing them to terrify you? What fears are you withholding from God?

Think about it. If you're gripped with fear about the future of your marriage, this is an indication that you don't completely trust God with your marriage. If you're overwhelmed with worry about how you will pay your bills, this reveals that you may not be trusting God to be your provider. If you're paralyzed with worry about the safety of your children, could it be that you aren't trusting God to keep them safe?

From my experience praying this prayer, God has often revealed my anxious thoughts and the fears fueling them. One of the first fears he revealed has also proven to be one of the most persistent. I'm terrified of failing. It started as a child playing baseball and feeling scared to death I'd strike out in front of my once professional-baseball-playing dad. As an adult, I'm afraid of striking out on my next sermon, my next project, or my responsibility to be a good dad. I'm scared to death to let people down, of not being enough, of not doing what needs to be done. I always feel inadequate.

In fact, as I'm typing the words on this page, I'm worried about my daughter's health. Mandy's twenty-three, married, and as gifted as anyone I know. Yet for almost three years now, she's been unable to function like a normal person. We've prayed more prayers than we could count. We've seen doctors across the nation. We've tried the most specific diets you could imagine. We've tried natural approaches and even some things that would make some people think we are crazy. Not only am I a Christian, I'm a pastor. I know I'm not supposed to worry. But when it's your own child, it's hard not to let your mind race in the wrong direction.

Which brings me back to why I wanted to write this book. With all my heart, I know the power of praying dangerous prayers. And I'm continually sick of my safe prayers. I can't stand another day of my self-centered Christianity. So this message burns within me. But I'm worried that I won't be able to get the idea from my heart onto the page. What if my writing isn't powerful enough? Isn't convincing? Isn't convicting? Doesn't move your heart?

Our fears matter. Because ultimately, our fears show how we're relying on our own efforts and not trusting in our Savior. The truth is we—you and I and everyone—are always inadequate. We're never enough. We're always weak. But here's the incredible thing: when we're weak, God's power is made perfect (see 2 Cor. 12:9).

> Our fears matter. Because ultimately, our fears show how we're relying on our own efforts and not trusting in our Savior.

Your greatest fear may point you to your best chance at making a difference in the world. You need God for every moment of every day. Everything you do of value is born out of his heart, his power, his grace.

To please God, to serve him, to honor him, to live for him,

you cannot be driven by fear. You must be led by faith. I've often said, the pathway to your greatest potential is often straight through your greatest fear. Faith will propel you forward. In fact, what God wants for you may be on the other side of what you fear the most. The apostle Paul encouraged his protégé Timothy to cling to faith by reminding him, "God has not given us a spirit of fear and timidity, but of power, love, and self-discipline" (2 Tim. 1:7 NLT).

> To please God, to serve him, to honor him, to live for him, you cannot be driven by fear. You must be led by faith.

Through the centuries, many Christians have believed that God's enemy, the devil, attempts to influence believers with lies. If you're afraid of failing, it could be that your spiritual enemy is trying to talk you out of doing what God has created you to do. So pray and step into your fear. Let God propel you forward by faith. Without faith, it's impossible to please God. Remind yourself that you love pleasing God more than you fear failing.

As you pray this dangerous prayer and he reveals what is keeping you from fully following him, don't miss out on experiencing his love. Soak in his extravagant grace. Enjoy the unconditional goodness of God poured out for you in the life of Christ. Remember, "perfect love drives out fear" (1 John 4:18).

As God reveals your fears, he will also build your faith. You need him. You need his presence. You need his power. You need his Spirit guiding you. You need his Word strengthening you.

Faith doesn't mean you don't get afraid. Faith means you don't let fear stop you.

What you fear the most shows you where you need to grow with God. What do you fear? What are your anxious thoughts?

What is God showing you?

Where do you need to grow in faith?

Trust him.

UNCOVER MY SINS

If David's prayer hasn't seemed dangerous enough already, then I'd like to gently warn you. It's about to get even more intense.

David was called "a man after God's own heart" (see 1 Sam. 13:14 and Acts 13:22). He was devoted to God's will and worshiped passionately, gave extravagantly, and led courageously. Yet he still made mistakes—big ones. Like you and like me, he was tempted to sin and didn't always make the right choice. Even after he knew the goodness of God and had walked with him for most of his life, David still blew it. And that's why he prayed this dangerous portion of the prayer: "Search me, God ... know my anxious thoughts. ... See if there is any offensive way in me" (Ps. 139:23–24).

Show me if I am doing anything that offends or hurts your heart.

Hearing God's response to this portion of the prayer can

be challenging. It's not easy because most of us are masters at rationalizing our wrong actions. If you're like me, you're good at accusing others, and equally good at excusing yourself. I can point out your faults but have a perfectly good explanation as to why I do anything that you might consider inappropriate. I'm good at doing what Jesus warned against in Matthew 7. I can point out the speck of sawdust in your eye all the while ignoring the log in my own eye.

> If you're like me, you're good at accusing others, and equally good at excusing yourself.

How do you hear from God about any offensive way in you? Let me suggest three things to consider as you are searching God's heart with this dangerous prayer.

First, consider what others have told you about *you*. Is there an area of your life, your habits, your relationships, or your actions that others have suggested needs to change? Is there some area of your life that is challenged by others? Have loved ones expressed concern for you, or asked you to consider getting help?

When I was in seminary and took a counseling class, my professor taught us a principle I'll never forget. She suggested that if more than two people that you love and trust suggest you have a problem, you should recognize that you have a problem and deal with it immediately.

Her wisdom stuck with me through the years. As you ask God to show you if you have any offensive ways, start with what others have mentioned to you. Is there something about your life that loved ones suggest is unhealthy or unwise?

Maybe some people have suggested that you play video games way too much. They are concerned that you have more to offer, that you are missing out on more important things in life.

Perhaps someone has suggested that you drink too much. Or have a problem with pain medication. Or overeating. If more than two trusted friends or family members have suggested this, maybe it's time to pause and pay attention.

Maybe you have had a bad run at dating. Your friends continue to remind you that you are always saying yes to the wrong kind of person. Rather than defending your actions, perhaps it's time to consider changing your patterns.

In recent years, I finally had to pause and recognize something that was out of whack in my life. Several people suggested that I was a slave to my mobile phone. My wife, Amy, was the loudest and most outspoken. My kids' sighs and rolled eyes spoke volumes as well.

Before I took their loving observation seriously, my defenses kicked in. The expert rationalizer emerged. *What I'm doing is important. To be a good pastor I have to be available to people. I'm leading a church and my opinion is important. My social media presence can be a good witness. I really need to see how my last Instagram post is performing and check to see if there are any comments needing my attention.*

You would think that hearing from Amy and my kids would be enough. But when a few people from the office mentioned it, my old seminary professor's advice started to echo in my brain. So I decided to pray, *Show me, God. See if there is an offensive way in me. Is this a problem?*

I was at my son's soccer game when God answered my prayer. I was responding to a text and missed my son's amazing corner kick that his teammate headed into the goal to take a 1–0 lead against the top-ranked team. Then late in the second half with the game tied 1–1 and a few minutes left to go, I missed my son's game-winning goal because I was checking on a social media post.

God showed me clearly: I was settling for a counterfeit reality and missing out on what mattered most. I was missing out on my life, losing precious moments with the people I love most.

What about you? Is there something others have been trying to help you see about yourself that needs to change? Proverbs 12:15 says, "The way of fools seems right to them, but the wise listen to advice." Maybe it's time to pause and listen. God may speak to you through those who love you most.

> Proverbs 12:15 says, "The way of fools seems right to them, but the wise listen to advice."

On top of considering what others have told you, also consider what you've rationalized. Is there something in your life that is wrong, but you continue to ignore God's gracious warning signals?

If I'm honest, my ability to rationalize sin is scary. Though it's kind of funny now, there is a story that couldn't illustrate this idea better. Years ago at church, I was playfully railing against people who drive down the shoulder during big traffic jams. Chances are you have seen this. Traffic is at a standstill on the highway and backed up for miles when inevitably there will be a driver who pulls onto the shoulder on the right side of the road and drives past everyone else who is following the rules. During that Sunday sermon, I joked about those people answering to God before he sends them straight to hell.

The very next day I was driving to the church office early on Monday morning. For some reason, there was more traffic than usual backed up about a half a mile in front of our church. I patiently waited, wondering why we weren't moving. After several minutes of no movement at all, I looked over to the right side. Our church owned all the land between where I sat stuck and the entrance to our church driveway. The land was still undeveloped and the grass was easy to drive on. I rationalized that the land belonged to the church so I had the right to drive on it. And off I went. Driving past other drivers on the side of the road.

Little did I know that I drove right by one of our church members named Mark Dawson. Beside him was his young son, Alex, who shouted out, "Daddy, there is one of those drivers that Pastor Craig hates!" He had barely finished his first sentence when he shouted out in shock and dismay, "Daddy! That guy *is* Pastor Craig!" Less than twenty-four hours after I had ranted about how driving on the shoulder is wrong, I did exactly the same thing.

Lord, show me if there is any offensive way in me.

Consider what you've rationalized. Is there an area of your life about which others have expressed concern? And you've defended yourself? It's no big deal. I can handle this. This is just how I cope. Besides, I'm not hurting anyone anyway. It's my life. Who are you to judge me? I don't have a problem. I'm fine. You just keep to your business and leave me to mine.

This is another reason why this dangerous prayer is not only important but imperative. We need God's help to see the sin that's difficult to see in the mirror. If we are not careful, we can end up like the people David described in Psalm 36. He powerfully stated, "In their own eyes they flatter themselves too much to detect or hate their sin. The words of their mouths are wicked and deceitful; they fail to act wisely or do good" (Ps. 36:2–3).

We need God's help to see the sin that's difficult to see in the mirror.

How often do we flatter ourselves? I'm not like them. I'm fine spiritually. I don't have a problem. Without even knowing it, our deceptive hearts deceive us into ignoring our own sin. And the rationalizations continue.

- There's nothing wrong with looking at porn. Everyone does it. Besides, I could be doing much worse. I'm not hurting anyone.
- I don't have a temper problem. I wouldn't yell at you if you didn't do what you do. It's not my fault you make me so mad.

- My drinking is not a problem. I just have a few beers to help me unwind. It's not like I'm chugging whiskey or something.
- I'm not gossiping. I can't help it that people tell me things. I'm just passing along information that's likely true. Besides, it helps others know how to pray.
- Gambling is not a problem for me. It's just entertainment. I can stop at any time.
- I'm not selfish. I just like nice things. I want what's mine. I've worked hard my whole life. I deserve a few good things in life.

King David knew a lot about rationalizing. We will never know the exact story he told himself before taking Bathsheba into his bed, then murdering her innocent husband, Uriah, to cover it up. (For the full story read 2 Sam. 11–12.) But knowing how our minds work, I'm guessing he told himself something like this: *I deserve some down time. I've fought and won many battles. Now I need to disconnect.*

Then while strolling on the roof of his palace to unwind, perhaps sipping on his favorite drink, the king notices a beautiful woman several doors over.

Wow… check that out. Who is that gal on the roof? I'm feeling pretty lonely. I'd love some company. I'd like to get to know her. Just find out about who she is. I won't do anything. I just need someone to talk to.

Then after commanding his servant to go get her and bring her to the palace, his rationalizations surely continued.

She is lonely. Her husband probably doesn't even have a clue what he has. I'm the king. I deserve a little extra attention. No one will ever find out. Besides, I've got my needs.

On and on. Step by step. David told himself lies stacked upon lies.

In my own life, I've learned that when I'm defensive, that's an indication I need to pay close attention and be open to what God wants to show me. If someone is suggesting a change in your life and you bark back, instead of barking, you would be wise to listen. If you sense that God is convicting you of something and you are quick to tell him why you don't need to change, this is a clear signal to pause and heed his warning.

I've found that the more convinced I am that I'm right about something, the more likely that I'm wrong.

I learned this the hard way, of course. As a young pastor, I had dozens of wise people approach me and tell me that I was occasionally too crude in my preaching. They were concerned that my humor was at best off-color, at worst inappropriate.

I didn't budge.

Little did they know, I had a strategy. As a guy who was turned off by overly religious, holier-than-thou preachers, I was going to show everyone I was a regular guy. I had fun like regular people. And I had a sense of humor that people would enjoy.

The problem was that my standard was connecting with people but not honoring God.

After dozens of people tried to help me see the error of my ways, finally one guy helped me see the light. After visiting over lunch for a few minutes, he tried a different approach to help me see my problems. He started by sincerely complimenting my preaching. He loved my passion. He recognized that I studied faithfully. He admired my courage to preach on tough subjects. Then he started to encourage me about my faith in God. He told me sincerely that he knew I loved people who needed Christ and that I wanted to honor Jesus in how I lived.

As he continued to build me up with his words, he told me that he knew that I knew many were concerned about my crude humor. This wise man told me that he trusted me and that if I had a problem, he knew I would listen to God. Rather than accusing me, he simply encouraged me. "Would you ask God to show you if this is something he would have you change?"

Because of his loving spirit, I agreed to ask God. Truthfully, I didn't plan on hearing anything different from God at all. God knew my heart. God understood my plan.

> Would you ask God to show you if this is something he would have you change?

So I simply prayed a dangerous prayer. "Show me if I'm wrong, God. Show me if I need to change."

Nothing happened.

Nothing at all.

Until the very next time I preached.

It happened to be "promotion weekend," when the kids in church move up into a new grade or class. On this weekend, my oldest daughter, Catie, had graduated from kids' church and was now old enough to worship in "big church" every week.

Several minutes into my message, I preached away with confidence and passion, glancing to the side to see my precious young daughter sitting next to Amy (who also thought my humor went too far). Right before I delivered a joke that some would have considered questionable, it dawned on me: *I don't want my daughter to hear this. I would never want her to say this.* And in one moment, God got through to me. They were right. I was wrong. I had been unknowingly crude, dishonoring God, and disrespectful to so many amazing people.

That place that I had been most sure that I was right was the place that I was most wrong.

Denying the truth doesn't change the facts.

I was sinning against my God, and it took praying a dangerous prayer to accept the painful truth.

LEAD ME

Are you ready to pray this dangerous prayer? Are you prepared to hear what God might show you as you do? Do you have the faith to ask and the courage to obey?

Search my heart, God.

Reveal my anxious thoughts.

See if there is any offensive way in me.

And lead me in the way everlasting.

Every phrase in this faith-filled cry to God is important. But it's incomplete without the final passionate prayer—lead me in the way everlasting.

We don't want God to just show us the impurity of our hearts. We want more than to simply know our fearful and anxious thoughts. We desire more than just knowing how we are offensive. We want God to lead us, to direct us, to guide us to become who he wants us to be.

Lead us in the way everlasting.

When you pause to pray this prayer and listen, God will speak to you. But don't take this prayer lightly. Don't pray it half-heartedly. This isn't a game or a sterile little spiritual exercise to help you have a better day. This is a soul-cleansing, heart-mending, eternity-altering prayer.

"Lead me."

As I reflect on my spiritual journey through this prayer, let me recap what God has been showing me.

1. Search my heart, God. God showed me my hypocrisy. I often show people the me I want them to see. My words honor God, but my heart can be far from him.

2. Know my anxious thoughts. I'm scared to death of not measuring up. I'm haunted by my insecurities. I'm paralyzed with fear that I don't have what it takes to please people.

3. See if there is any offensive way in me. Time and again, I've put the approval of people ahead of the approval of God. I've battled with wanting to be liked by people more than wanting to express my love for God.

4. Lead me. And this is where the rubber meets the road. This is where things get real. This is where genuine, Spirit-filled, life-altering change becomes possible.

When I put all these portions of this one dangerous prayer together and listen to what God wants to show me, it becomes clear: I've consistently battled with putting the approval of people ahead of the approval of God. This is perhaps my deepest inner spiritual flaw. It's sin. And it's keeping me from serving God with my whole heart. Why? Because becoming obsessed with what people think about me is the quickest way to forget what God thinks about me. Being obsessed with the approval of others is, in a word, idolatry.

I've consistently battled with putting the approval of people ahead of the approval of God.

So I'm asking God to make me different. Stronger. More confident in Christ. More secure in his love and calling. And it's working. My preaching is bolder. My leadership is sharper. My sensitivity to his Spirit is stronger. And as I care less about what people think, I'm more passionate about what God thinks. I'm less in love with this world, and my mind is more focused on eternity.

Lead me.

Pray it.

Search me, God.

Know my anxious thoughts.

See if there are any offensive ways in me.

And lead me in the way everlasting.

As you do, listen for what God says. Watch for what he shows you. See how he connects the dots and points to your deepest need.

But don't be discouraged. Be full of faith. Discovering your deepest need is a gift. It's an opportunity. It's a blessing.

Because your deepest need becomes a gift when it moves you to depend on Christ.

This is what I'm learning from my daughter, Mandy. As I mentioned earlier, she's been struggling with chronic fatigue, fibromyalgia, and several other complicated, life-altering issues. When I told her that I was proud of the way she was enduring the sickness, Mandy stopped me midsentence.

Your deepest need becomes a gift when it moves you to depend on Christ.

"Daddy," she said, gently correcting me, "I've chosen not to use the word *enduring*. Enduring is a passive response to something that is happening." I hung on every word as my precious daughter gave her pastor-daddy a spiritual lesson. She continued, "I'm embracing this whole situation. With everything in me, I believe God is using it to help me know him better and help others know him too."

Wiping away the tears, I had to acknowledge God had drawn her even closer. And rather than letting her physical condition rob her of the chance to make a difference, when Mandy can't go out, she just records encouraging messages from home. As of the writing of this book, she has more than ten thousand people who subscribe to her YouTube channel to hear about her hope and faith in Christ.

God will do the same for you.

Wherever you are weak, his strength is there.

Wherever you are hurting, his comfort is available.

When you are tempted, his grace will give you a way out.

Let your fears drive you to God. The fear of God is the only cure for the fear of people.

If you battle with lust, let God's Word renew your mind.

If you are tripping over pride, humble yourself and God will lift you up.

If you are hiding a secret sin, find forgiveness by confessing it to God and healing by confessing it to trustworthy people.

Ask God to show you the truth. Because the truth will set you free.

Are you tired of boring, safe, sterile prayers? Are you stuck in a spiritual rut? Is your faith fat? Your passion low? Are you hungry for more? And ready to obey?

Then venture out into the deep waters of communication with God. Open your heart to healing from a divine God. Step into the beauty of God's forgiveness and grace. Seek his unfailing, unconditional, and unquenchable love. And have the courage to pray this dangerous prayer. But don't just pray it. Respond to what he shows you. Step through your greatest fear and into faith. Embrace your deepest need and let it drive you to depend on Christ.

Are you ready?

"Search me, Lord."

PART 2

BREAK ME

And when [Jesus] had given thanks, he broke [the bread] and said, "This is my body, which is for you; do this in remembrance of me."

—1 CORINTHIANS 11:24

BREAK ME

Years ago, David Wilkerson wrote a runaway bestselling book called *The Prayer of Jabez*. It focused on a couple of Bible verses in the Old Testament. If you've never heard of this guy, Jabez, it's no surprise. He's mentioned only three times in the Bible, so we don't know a lot of details about him. While we're told he was honorable (1 Chron. 4:9), the name Jabez actually means "he causes pain." His mother named him Jabez because his birth had caused such pain (v. 9). Most Bible scholars believe that his birth must have been exceptionally painful or traumatic for his mother to give him such a name.

Perhaps that's why Jabez prayed this particular prayer: "Oh, that you would bless me and enlarge my territory! Let your hand be with me, and keep me from harm so that I will be free from pain" (v. 10). We're told God granted him this request.

When I read Wilkerson's book, I was struck by the simplicity of this prayer. Bless me. Enlarge my territory. Let your hand be with me. Keep me from harm so that I will be free from pain. This is the type of prayer we all want to pray, right? Bless me. (Give me more of what I want.) Protect me. (Keep away from me what I don't want.) Makes sense, right?

While I've prayed different versions of this prayer too many times to count, I've been forced to come to terms with its limitations. This prayer—although scriptural and useful—is focused on what we want, not necessarily what God wants. It's safe. It's comfortable. Someone could even argue that it's somewhat shortsighted—even selfish.

Keep me from harm and free from pain makes sense. Who wants hardship? Who wants to struggle? But I wonder if we might as well be praying, "God, don't let me grow. Don't let me get stronger. Don't allow me to trust you more." Even though trials are never fun or easy to endure, God can often use them for his purposes. In fact, James, the half-brother of Jesus, was bold enough to tell us we should be *thankful* for the way God uses hardship to perfect us: "Consider it pure joy, my brothers and sisters, whenever you face trials of many kinds, because you know that the testing of your faith produces perseverance. Let perseverance finish its work so that you may be mature and complete, not lacking anything" (James 1:2–4).

If we pray only for protection from trials, then we rob ourselves of our future maturity. "Lord, keep me free from pain" feels like the right thing to pray—and often is. But if that's our only desire, our biggest priority, then we may miss the perseverance that our trials produce. "God, protect me from harm" seems wise to pray—and can be. But it's the challenges in life that help us mature and draw us closer to Christ.

It's fine to pray for safety and blessings, but what if you want more? What if you desire power from the Holy Spirit, strength from heaven, unshakable faith, genuine intimacy with your Father?

If we pray only for protection from trials, then we rob ourselves of our future maturity.

Instead of just asking God to keep you safe, give you more, and protect your life, you may have to ask God to break you.

BURST YOUR BUBBLE

At the ripe old age of twenty-seven, I felt called by God to start a new church. My wife, Amy, shared my vision, so we dreamed together and moved forward with a plan. We chose a name for our new church and filed the paperwork. We recruited friends who had already expressed interest in joining us and printed invitations for others we hoped to enlist as we got our new church off the ground.

To say that we were idealistic would be an understatement. With way more faith than wisdom, I envisioned how it would be. I'd preach powerful messages. The atmosphere would be electric, with vibrant worship and dynamic music. Crowds of people would gather. Lives would be changed. God would be honored. The city would be different. And we would live happily ever after.

With my plan clearly mapped out in my mind, I sat across the table at breakfast with one of my mentors, Gary Walter.

Having helped many young church planters start thriving and life-giving churches, Gary was considered an expert. With fatherly concern and the wisdom of a spiritual veteran, he generously helped give me direction and perspective. When he asked about my plans, I barely touched my eggs and bacon as I boldly explained my vision.

But before I could convince Gary of how our little band of faithful people would grow into a worldwide movement, he stopped me midsentence. It wasn't rude or abrupt—in fact, just the opposite. I'll never forget the loving, fatherly, and pastoral tone of his voice as he gently asked if he could tell me something. As I nodded, he said, "I have one promise for you and one promise only." Then he paused for an awkwardly long time, letting his statement sink in.

I leaned in, holding my breath, anticipating what he'd say next. One promise? If he had only one, then it had to be good. What was it? Maybe Gary would promise me that God would open the door for me to declare the good news of Jesus to thousands of people in countries around the world. That God would use me, use our church, to do more than I could ever imagine. That the world would be different and better because of our efforts through the church.

"My only promise for you is this: God will break you."

Gary's words, slow and deliberate and kind, crushed me with their weight.

I glared back. My expression likely displayed a mixture of betrayal and confusion. *What do you mean? God will break me?*

What kind of promise is that? Why would God want to break me?
What kind of mentor tells you that? And what kind of God would
allow that to happen?

What happened in the next few minutes after that statement is a blur. I don't remember if Gary continued talking. Or
if I argued. Or if I just sat there and let his prophetic declara-
tion shatter my bones. I just remember the stunned emotion of
hearing those words. That was the last thing I wanted to hear.
To believe. To happen. I mean, I was obeying God and doing
what he wanted me to do, right? Shouldn't the opposite be
true? Shouldn't God reward me or at least *not* try to break me?

As much as I wanted to fight Gary's observation, I knew
what he said was true.

He didn't burst my bubble—the truth did.

God would break me.

And, at least in theory, I would be better because of it.

If I survived.

Once I regained my stability, I remember Gary explaining why this was the path that I would have to travel. Gary
quoted A. W. Tozer, who said, "It is
doubtful whether God can bless a
man greatly until he has hurt him
deeply." I remember thinking then
what I think now: *I'm not sure I like*
that idea. Did I even believe it? Is
that the price I'd have to pay for God to use me greatly? Isn't
there an easier way?

> "It is doubtful whether God
> can bless a man greatly until
> he has hurt him deeply."
>
> —A. W. TOZER

Gary reminded me that God loved me. He always has my best interests in mind. But for me to be wholly useful to him, I'd have to be empty of myself. God would have to break me of pride, of self-confidence, of self-sufficiency. And God would also have to break me of things that I didn't even know needed to be removed from my life.

To be wholly useful to God, we have to be empty of self.

If I wanted to be used by God for his glory, then there was no way around it.

I would have to surrender to God.

God would need to break me.

STATUS QUO

When I think about praying this prayer, "Lord, break me," I think about the experience Amy and I once had in our small group. On a blustery, cold Wednesday night in January, we sat around a warm and cozy room with seven or eight other couples talking about this exact dangerous prayer. I was struck by the contrast, if not irony, of the topic we were there to discuss. Outside it was probably 15 degrees Fahrenheit, with the windchill close to zero. Despite the miserable evening outside, we sat in a comfortable living room on leather sofas with a warm fire blazing in the corner. With stomachs full of homemade chili and cornbread, we now turned to what it would mean to pray such a dangerous prayer.

We agreed we all *wanted* to pray it—and mean it—but couldn't deny being afraid of the consequences. The first woman who spoke took the possibility seriously but acknowledged her struggle. A loving wife and mother of four, she had followed Jesus faithfully since she was a sophomore in high school. She served in the kids' ministry at church, tithed faithfully, helped foster children, attended a weekly Bible study, and often volunteered to pray out loud in groups.

But when confronted with the option of asking God to break her, she refused. "Sorry, but I've got to be honest," she said. "I don't want to ask God to break me. I'm afraid of what will happen. I'm a mom with four kids. I love them too much. Asking God to break me is simply too scary for me to ever pray. What if I get sick or depressed or pulled away from my family?"

Most other people in the small group nodded in agreement. One by one, each person explained why they were hesitant, afraid, and unwilling to pray that dangerous prayer. So we continued talking about it, each of us identifying and justifying why it was okay not to pray such a dangerous prayer. All of us Christians, lounging comfortably near the fire, sipping on warm coffee with soft praise music playing in the background.

At the end of our time together, though no one prayed it out loud, the cry of our hearts seemed clear: "Keep us comfortable, God. Keep us warm and cozy. Don't break us—it would hurt too much. Please, just keep things going smoothly."

What are we losing by clinging to our comfort?

But my question then remains the same for all of us today: what are we losing by clinging to our comfort?

What are we missing out on because we're so committed to avoiding pain and discomfort?

Could there be something on the other side of suffering that somehow makes it worthwhile?

Could breaking be as necessary to our growth as it is to a baby bird cracking away the shell around it? As a butterfly coming out of the cocoon?

Could being broken release us for more than we can even imagine?

BROKEN AND RELEASED

Looking back, I now see why my small group reacted the way most of us do when we consider praying something so bold, crazy really, as "break me." But I also suspect that most of us don't realize that by playing it safe, we risk missing something far more precious than our security and comfort. We don't realize what blessings might be on the other side of God's breaking.

I see these blessings emerge in two powerful scenes from Christ's life. Both are described in the book of Mark, curiously enough, back to back. While they may appear unrelated on the surface, there is a very consistent theme. Something is broken so that something else can be released.

> We don't realize what blessings might be on the other side of God's breaking.

In the first example, Mark describes the dramatic scene in which an unwanted visitor crashes a dinner party where Jesus was a guest. The visitor was a prostitute, and times haven't changed much about how others view them. Most women hold them in contempt. Most men view them as objects for transactions or judge them or both. But we must keep in mind, no woman grows up aspiring to be a lady of the evening, as my grandmother used to call them. In most cases, desperation drives a person to sell their body in order to survive. Many likely feel powerless, trapped without any options to improve their life.

The same was true in Jesus' day. If a young woman became a prostitute, it was only because she was desperate beyond measure. She would have seen no other choice. Perhaps she was a single mom and was afraid her children would go hungry. Maybe she had been sold into slavery and saw no way out. Perhaps she'd been abused for her entire life, had no self-worth, and simply didn't believe she was worthy of anything more than using her body to survive.

We don't know a lot of details about the woman in the story. But we do know what she did for a living. And we do know that somewhere, sometime, somehow, she encountered the love of Christ. We don't know exactly when she met Jesus or what he said to her. We don't know if others observed her transformation or if she experienced God's love alone somewhere on a dirt road. The only thing we know for sure is that she met Christ. And she knew with certainty that Jesus was different.

In some way, at some time, he showed her unconditional

love when she had known only abuse. He treated her with dignity. He showed her respect. He honored her when others heaped shame. Jesus would have shown her the same love, same grace, same mercy that he offered to every repentant sinner that he'd ever encountered. Though she would have been full of shame, he helped her feel worthy. Though she would have felt worthless, he showed her that she had value. Though she was guilty of sin, Jesus offered her grace.

So this woman wanted to do something to show her gratitude. Knowing Jesus and his disciples were at the home of Simon the Leper, she went in to deliver her thanks to her Redeemer. Whether premeditated or spontaneous, it's unclear, but the value of her extraordinary offering goes without saying. She likely brought her most precious possession, an expensive jar of exotic perfume, and in an act of unbridled worship and devotion, "she broke the jar and poured the perfume on his head" (Mark 14:3).

At first glance, this may not sound like much of a big deal. So she broke open a jar of Chanel? So what? But her audience immediately recognized the significance of this gift on multiple levels. First, there was the value of the perfume. This rare and expensive treasure would have cost someone about a year's worth of wages to purchase.

Think about that. How much do you make in a year? Now imagine, in one moment, with one single display of worship, giving that whole amount to Jesus. That is what this woman did. She broke the bottle and gave it all.

How much do you make in a year? Now imagine, in one moment, with one single display of worship, giving that whole amount to Jesus. That is what this woman did. She broke the bottle and gave it all.

Remember, this woman was not doing a job that she loved. One year of wages equals one year of shame. One year of humiliation. One year of sin. How many horrible encounters did she have in that year? How many men used her and despised her? And yet she broke open the bottle and worshiped Jesus.

This sudden gift shocked some of the people in the room. Stunned, they barked indignantly to one another, "'Why this waste of perfume? It could have been sold for more than a year's wages and the money given to the poor.' And they rebuked her harshly" (Mark 14:4–5). Maybe you and I would have reacted the same way. It seems so wasteful, a crazy stunt.

But it wasn't just a stunt. The magnitude of this selfless act of devotion didn't stop at the monetary value of the jar's contents.

At that time, perfume was so rare that everyday women never thought of buying or wearing perfume. It simply wasn't feasible. It cost way too much. So who would be willing to drop the big bucks for fragrance? Women like this one. Some theologians believe the only women who wore perfume were "the women of the streets." The fragrance was a form of advertising. Those who wore perfume were sending a bold and fragrant message, "I'm available . . . for a price."

So when this woman broke open the bottle and poured out the valuable cologne, she wasn't just parting with the money she had earned. She was parting with her past, her profession, her livelihood. The perfume not only represented the work she used to do; it also represented what she could use to stir up future "business." When she broke the bottle, she burned her bridges. No going back. She poured out all the perfume on Jesus, symbolizing that she would give him all of her life.

Jesus, here's my life.
It's all yours.
I'm holding nothing back.

She broke the jar and she poured it all out.

Released it. Surrendered herself.

Her act communicated more than any words.

Jesus, here's my life.

It's all yours.

I'm holding nothing back.

"Lord, you can have it all."

CHAPTER 2.5

BREAKING BREAD

From breaking perfume bottles, Mark shifts our attention to another scene where Jesus himself broke something. It wasn't a jar of cologne but rather bread at the table he shared with his disciples. And this wasn't just any meal but the one that's become known as the Last Supper, the final gathering of Jesus, prior to his death, with all his closest and most trusted friends. At this intimate meal, Jesus offered them bread and wine, using the grain and grape as visual aids to foreshadow his imminent suffering and death. Then he invited his disciples to celebrate the same symbolic meal in remembrance of him for years to come: "While they were eating, Jesus took bread, and when he had given thanks, he broke it and gave it to his disciples, saying, 'Take it; this is my body.' Then he took a cup, and when he had given thanks, he gave it to them, and they all drank from it. 'This is my blood of the covenant, which is poured out for many,' he said to them" (Mark 14:22–24).

Notice exactly what Jesus did. He broke bread and explained that this breaking symbolized what would happen to him, to his body. It would be broken, bruised, and crushed. His back would bear the stripes of brutal scourging. His face would be bloodied by fists, and his head pierced by a garland of thorns. His hands and feet would be nailed to beams of wood. He would hang as the crowd spit on him. Mocked him. Cursed at him. Jesus would be surrounded by two guilty thieves—although he did nothing wrong. Jesus would fight to gain his breath. Cry out to God in pain. Forgive those who hung him. And give his life for us.

Like the bread he broke at the table, Jesus' body would be broken. Then after sharing the bread with his disciples, Jesus held up a cup of wine. Jesus slowly, deliberately, and lovingly explained that the wine represented his blood. Before long, he would spill his blood to cover the sins of guilty men. He was the Lamb of God. The sacrificial Lamb would be slain.

As Jesus looked into the eyes of those he had chosen, he knew that Peter would deny him and Judas would betray him. Yet he continued to love them and explained that he must offer his life (Mark 14:12–31). As he had told them before, "There is no greater love than to lay down one's life for one's friends" (John 15:13 NLT).

"There is no greater love than to lay down one's life for one's friends" (John 15:13 NLT).

His body would be broken, and his blood would be spilled.

Luke's Gospel described the very same meal but noted something that Mark didn't mention. Luke said, "And [Jesus] took bread, gave thanks and broke it, and gave it to them, saying, 'This is my body given for you; do this in remembrance of me'" (Luke 22:19).

Almost all Bible scholars agree that Jesus' instruction to "do this" provides believers a way to remember, honor, and celebrate his death and resurrection. As a result, for centuries, followers of Christ have gathered and shared in this act of breaking bread, offering wine, and partaking of both in an act of worship. Known as Holy Communion, the Lord's Supper, or the Eucharist, this partaking of bread and wine helps us to recall the extraordinary sacrifice, the price Jesus paid, that we could be forgiven and in eternal fellowship with the Father.

But some scholars believe, and I agree, that Jesus' instruction to "do this" included more than a simple and short act, or ritual, involving bread and wine. Some believe that Jesus' "do this" also refers to how we are to live. We don't just remember Jesus during Holy Communion at church; we remember him in how we live our lives daily. Because Jesus' body was broken, because his blood was poured out for us, we too should live daily for him, broken and poured out.

This may not sound appealing at first glance. Who wants to be "broken" and "poured out"? That sounds painful at best, miserable at worst. But it's in the giving of our lives that we find true joy. Rather than pursuing our will, we surrender to his. Instead of trying to fill our lives with all that we want, we empty our lives to make a difference in the lives of others.

Our friends Jerome and Shanna have taken in so many children in need that I'm not even sure they could tell you how many hurting kids they've helped. In the process, they've cried countless nights. They've ached with disappointment. And they've given until it hurts. But in their selfless giving, they've found joy. And when I asked them if they would do any of it differently, without any hesitation, they said in unison, "No way. We've been given so much. Now it's our time to give back." Jerome and Shanna know firsthand the blessing of living broken and poured out.

> Who wants to be "broken" and "poured out"? That sounds painful at best, miserable at worst. But it's in the giving of our lives that we find true joy.

It's difficult to imagine what the disciples must have thought and felt in that moment with God's Son gathered around the table. They didn't want him to die. Most probably they didn't believe that he would. So I wonder if memories of things Jesus said previously flooded through their minds. "Oh . . . wow . . . now it makes sense. Jesus told us that if we wanted to be his disciple we would have to deny ourselves, take up our cross, and follow him" (see Matt. 16:24).

We too are to die to ourselves, so we can live for him. Broken and poured out.

Then the disciples might have remembered what Jesus

said after inviting them to take up their cross. It was so confusing then. It didn't make sense in that context walking along just talking to Jesus. Now, in light of the moment, it made more sense. Jesus said, "For whoever wants to save their life will lose it, but whoever loses their life for me will find it" (Matt. 16:25). Jesus isn't inviting us to a life of comfort and ease, but one of surrender and sacrifice. Our highest desire shouldn't be for our will to be done, but for his will to be done. And Jesus is inviting us to die to our own lives, so we can live moment by moment, day by day—for him. To leave our cozy living rooms and safe prayers in order to know what it means to be broken for the sake of others.

> "For whoever wants to save their life will lose it, but whoever loses their life for me will find it" (Matt. 16:25).

What if when Jesus said "do this," he wasn't just talking about a ritual that we do occasionally at church? What if he was also inviting us to be broken and poured out daily? What if he was inviting us to a life of humility, sacrifice, generosity, and joy? What if, instead of praying, "God watch over me, protect me, and bless me," we invited God to do something deeper in our lives?

What if we recognized that burdens can, with God's help, become blessings? What if we embraced the truth that problems can make us stronger? That trials can strengthen our faith? That hurting can make us more compassionate for the plight of others? That suffering can draw us closer to Christ?

What if we had the courage, the audacity, the faith to pray, "God, break me"? What if we too lived broken and poured-out lives for Christ?

JACK-IN-THE-BOX

Back when I started our church, my mentor Gary had made me the boldest promise I never wanted to hear: "God will break you."

He was so confident in his prophetic statement that I never doubted him. Not only was he confident that God would eventually break me, but he was even more confident that God would use it. The "breaking" would make me better. It would sharpen my leadership. Deepen my faith. Increase my intimacy with Jesus.

So I started praying one of the most dangerous prayers anyone can pray. "God, I trust you so much. I know that you love me, that you are always working in me. If you want to do something more in me, then do it. If it's painful, then I welcome the pain. If you want to use trials to make me stronger, build my faith, make me closer to you, then use them. God, do whatever it takes to free me from my love for this world. To crucify my love of comfort. God, break me."

Although God doesn't say yes to all my prayers, somehow, I knew he was likely to answer this one. Believing "the breaking" would come, I braced myself. Surely it would happen. Now. Today. Or if not today, then tomorrow. Soon. God would break me. Though I trusted him, every day I waited and wondered. Would it be today?

> God, do whatever it takes to free me from my love for this world. To crucify my love of comfort. God, break me.

The suspense and dread about killed me. Remember those old jack-in-the-box toys you played with as a kid? You'd crank the little lever on the side of a tiny box as creepy music played. Round and round it went, and even though you didn't know when it would happen, you knew it was only seconds away. It would happen. At some moment, Jack would suddenly pop out of the box and scare the pants off you. (On a side note, why did anyone think that terror-in-a-box would make a good toy for toddlers?) That's what I felt like. Every day, the lever was turning. The music was playing. And when I least expected it, the box would spring open. And God would break me.

I had heard that starting a church was difficult. Everyone who told me that was correct. Even though we experienced so many good things, blessings, and lives changed, the pain of the weight, the hard work, and the sacrifices often felt unbearable.

A few months in, our church lost the facility we were renting and had no place to meet. *God, what are you doing?* Then a news reporter wrote a scathing article about me that questioned my motives and created rumors and gossip that hurt my family. *God, why did you allow that to happen?* The workload was crushing. The hours grueling. The burden overwhelming. *God, I don't know if I will make it.*

As a young pastor, I made leadership mistakes that hurt people. Close friends got mad and left the church. I had to let staff members go. One was a close friend. That felt like a death. One was a family member. That felt worse than a death.

As each painful event unfolded, I'd call Gary and ask him, "Am I broken yet?" Each time Gary would gently tell me, "Not yet."

After several rounds of essentially the same conversation, Gary eventually told me, "Craig, when you are broken, you will know it. There will be no question. You will not have to ask."

> When you are broken, you will know it. There will be no question. You will not have to ask.

He was right.

BREAKING BAD

My jack-in-the-box finally popped up in a way that was both undeniable and far worse than anything I could have anticipated. My best friend in our church during those first years was a guy I will call Jason. When we started Life.Church, Jason left the church he was pastoring and moved to our city to help us in our church. Since we were too small to add staff and Jason was sorting out a few things in his life, he worked another job and we dreamed about his joining our staff one day in the near future. He quickly became my closest friend, confidante, and ministry partner.

But as most people do, Jason had some secrets. No one knew it at the time, but he had done something that left him feeling like his back was against the wall. Trying to maneuver from that position, he made a bad decision that I know he regretted. When I found out about it, I had no choice but to talk to him about it. His decision betrayed my trust and wounded our friendship. When I asked him about what he did, at first he denied it. Then with nowhere to hide, he became defensive and started yelling at me. He said some harsh words to me, and I responded back just as harshly. Jason stormed out of the room, got in his car, and sped off angrily.

The next Sunday, I wasn't surprised when Jason didn't show up for church. And I didn't blame him. He had made a very bad mistake and then said some things he shouldn't have said. He was hot. I was hurt. But even though the betrayal was significant and I felt both betrayed and angry, Jason was still my best friend. I knew that he'd calm down. We'd eventually talk it out. We'd forgive. We'd forget. And we'd move on.

But that healing conversation never happened.

About two weeks later, I had just finished preaching a message titled "Loving Those You Don't Like." Jason naturally came to mind, so on the drive home from church, I told Amy that I was going to call him that night and try to make things right between us. Yes, he'd hurt me, as well as many others, but he was my best friend. He wasn't perfect. Neither was I. It wasn't right to leave this distance lingering between us.

At home I was just about to pick up our landline phone when I noticed the indicator light blinking on our answering machine. When I pressed play, I heard Jason's wife sobbing. Through tear-choked cries, she said that Jason was dead. He had taken his life.

BOUND BY BROKENNESS

Gary told me that I would know when I was broken. That I wouldn't need to ask anyone. At that moment listening to my best friend's widow, I knew it without a doubt. Life would be different from this moment onward. I would never be the same.

But I wasn't the only one. Everyone close to Jason suffered and grieved and ached the same way. We were all broken, not only by his loss but by the circumstances around his passing. The next few days were a blur. We did the best we could to comfort each other, all the while trying to help Jason's family make major decisions.

After the tragedy, Jason's family never went back to the house where they found him. His wife and two kids moved in with us during their transition. We cried until the middle of the night and fell asleep when we were too exhausted to cry any more tears.

The days after someone dies are always odd. While you're

grieving, you also have to make plans for a funeral—a time to celebrate the love you just lost. Several days later, I officiated at the funeral. It was standing room only. Through my deep grief, I somehow tried to offer hope to those grieving alongside me.

Though no one there knew it, the last words Jason and I had spoken to each other were words we'd both forever regret. He had done wrong. Sinned. Lied. And betrayed God and me. But I didn't care any more about that betrayal. That was only a moment in time. A bad decision made by a desperate man who didn't see any other way.

No matter what he had done, I knew I should have acted sooner to mend our friendship. My heart had hardened and my stubborn pride and wounded ego got in the way of forgiving him and focusing on how I could help him. Flooded by guilt, I cried for what felt like days straight. The questions poured through my mind. *Why didn't he tell me he was in trouble? Why didn't he open up? In hindsight, there were so many signs of his distress. Why didn't I see it? Why did our last conversation have to be so terrible? Why didn't I reach out to him earlier?*

The following Sunday, I tried to preach. Though I had a sermon planned and started it, within a few minutes I knew there was no way that I'd ever get through it. So in front of a small crowd of people, I broke down sobbing. In one of the most publicly transparent moments of my life, I talked through all the pain and brokenness that we'd experienced since starting the church.

Before Jason's death, I was hurting. Exhausted. Overwhelmed. Scared.

After his death, I was simply wrecked. Shattered. Broken. Scarred.

Through tears, I told the church I felt guilty. Guilty that I hadn't reached out to Jason. Guilty that I hadn't done more. Guilty that I didn't know he was hurting. But my guilt reached far beyond Jason's tragedy. I felt guilty that I hadn't been a better dad because I was focusing so much on our growing church. And guilty that I hadn't been a better pastor because I was trying so hard to be enough for my wife and kids.

No matter how hard I tried, I simply wasn't enough.

I told the church that I felt broken and needed more than just prayer. I needed love. Grace. I needed them as friends. And I needed more of God than I had known in the past.

On that day, something changed in our young church. It went from being a small crowd of people gathering to a church family, a real grace-filled community. When I asked for support, almost everyone left their seats and came forward to pray, to cry, and to worship. Some people kneeled. Some people lifted their hands to heaven. Some people put their hands on our shoulders to pray for me and our family. We had all experienced the loss.

We were broken together.

It's easy to impress people with our strengths, but real

connections are forged through our shared weaknesses. We may impress people with what we can do. But we connect in our common struggles. This is one of the blessings of brokenness. We may fight to be strong. Show our best when posting selfies. And never let them see us down. But when we are broken together, bonding goes deeper than we can imagine—especially in the family of God. Just as persecution always unites, strengthens, and emboldens Christians who suffer together, so does brokenness create a bond that stands the test of time.

> It's easy to impress people with our strengths, but real connections are forged through our shared weaknesses.

What if rather than avoiding brokenness we embraced it? Welcomed it? And even prayed for it?

"God, break me."

CHAPTER 2.9

BLESSED BY BROKENNESS

For twenty-five years, I've had the same workout partner. His real name is John, but I call him Paco because, well, Paco seems like a better name for a workout partner. Even though Paco is older than I am, he's one tough dude. I've never seen him throw a punch and he's too kind to ever insult someone, but I have no doubt if push came to shove, I'd want him on my side in a street fight.

You might guess that Paco and I don't cry together.

We don't talk much about our feelings.

We're workout partners, not crying buddies.

But then something happened. Paco suddenly began experiencing severe ringing in his ears, and that's when I saw a different side of my tough buddy than I'd ever seen before. I didn't know much about tinnitus, but once I saw Paco suffer, I learned what a terrible ordeal it can be. For some, this constant ringing never stops. And there is no cure. For the more severe

97

cases (like Paco's), I understand it's like a train driving through your brain. Twenty-four hours a day. Every day.

Although there are some devices you can use, the pain for many is unbearable. Tragically, Paco had one of the worst cases his doctors had ever seen.

After traveling to the top experts and specialists, Paco got the best advice from a fellow tinnitus sufferer. The guy explained that the noise would never go away. And the only way you can endure it is to get closer to God than you've ever been and pour out your life serving other people.

Sounds crazy, doesn't it? Just suck it up and smile as you act like everything's okay. I remember when Paco told me about this guy's advice. It seemed trite. Useless. But Paco hadn't seen another person with severe tinnitus function as well as this man. So with nothing to lose, he tried it.

Daily, he pressed into God like he never had before. Reading God's living Word. Meditating on his truth and love. Worshiping. Praying. Fasting. John and his wife, Jennifer, started a small group and began pouring into others. They "adopted" a single mom and her kids and started serving them selflessly. And in giving their lives away, the roaring in the brain never got better, but somehow John started getting better. The pain didn't lessen, but John's joy increased.

At the gym one day we were trying to work out. John explained to me that tinnitus is the worst pain he could ever imagine. And yet, by God's grace, he'd never been closer to God than he was in that moment. He told me that in brokenness, he found joy.

I'm not sure if he started to get misty-eyed first or if it was me. But there in front of everyone in the gym, two lifelong friends couldn't hold back our tears.

In the brokenness and pouring out of his life, John found hope. In the middle of his worst pain, he discovered a peace from heaven that he didn't have the words to explain. I had discovered it for myself. But now I saw it in him. In our brokenness, we often experience God's greatest blessings.

In our brokenness, we often experience God's greatest blessings.

I'll admit, it takes tremendous faith to pray this prayer. It requires divine boldness. And I understand why many wouldn't ever ask for brokenness. But on the other side of fully trusting God, there is a blessing that cannot be found in comfort and ease.

When Gary told me that I'd be broken, I panicked. I wanted to avoid it at any cost. But had I tried to avoid the pain, I would have missed the blessings.

The apostle Paul cried out desperately to God for healing and deliverance from some unknown trial. In three different seasons, Paul begged, pleaded, and petitioned God to take it away. But when God said no, Paul discovered something he would have missed otherwise.[*]

God's grace was enough.

---

[*] You can read about Paul begging for deliverance from something he called a "thorn in my flesh" in 2 Corinthians 12:5–8. But also note that in 2 Corinthians 12:9–10, Paul says that even though the thorn is difficult to endure, he thanks God for it and realizes that when he is weak, God makes him strong.

Who does God most often use? God uses those who are broken and dependent on him.

During the Last Supper, Peter listened as Jesus explained that his body would be broken. Just a little while later, after Jesus had been arrested, Peter experienced his deepest breaking. Three times Peter denied even knowing Christ. On the third time, the Bible says someone asked Peter if he was with Jesus. "Peter replied, 'Man, I don't know what you're talking about!' Just as he was speaking, the rooster crowed. The Lord turned and looked straight at Peter" (Luke 22:60–61).

God uses those who are broken and dependent on him.

For years, I didn't notice that last part: "The Lord turned and looked straight at Peter."

Peter denied knowing Jesus. Jesus saw the denial. And their eyes met. Can you imagine the shame, the sorrow, the brokenness Peter felt? But then when Peter experienced the grace of Jesus after the resurrection, no one was better prepared to preach on the day of Pentecost. God chose Peter to be a foundational part of his church on earth. To tell others to turn from their sins. Because Peter had turned from his.

Years later, when Peter was asked to deny Christ, this time he refused. When the enemies of Christ wanted to crucify Peter on a cross, tradition tells us that he said he was unwilling to die as his Savior died. Instead, he asked to be crucified upside down. The same man who cowered in fear stood boldly in faith. He was a different man.

Peter was broken and poured out.

We may not be broken like Peter, or even like each other, but we will all face moments in life when we have a choice to make. When Gary told me I'd be broken, at first I fought to avoid the idea. As my trust and faith in God grew, not only did I accept it, but I also found the courage to pray for it. But there was something about brokenness that I didn't understand.

True brokenness before God isn't a one-time event; it's a daily decision. Paul said, "I die daily" (1 Cor. 15:31 NKJV). What does that mean? Every day, he chose to crucify his own desires so he could live fully for God's.

> True brokenness before God isn't a one-time event; it's a daily decision.

We are each called to die daily. To be broken and poured out. To become dependent on God's Spirit. To rely on him for our comfort, our guidance, our source of power.

Being broken isn't just a moment in time born out of a painful event. It's a daily choice to die to pride. To crucify lust. To destroy selfishness. Rather than living a life of ease, it's a choice to live a life of faith.

You might experience it when you do what's right, yet you are criticized by those who don't understand. Or when you respond with love, instead of anger, to someone who attacks you. Or when you faithfully do something you believe God directed you to do, even when it doesn't make a lot of sense and even when your coworkers mock you.

If you don't want to pray this dangerous prayer, then don't. Many people wouldn't blame you. I sure won't.

But if you have the courage to pray it, get ready. Get ready to know God, and be known by God, in a way you've not experienced before.

If you are struggling financially, fall on God and trust him for his provision. If your life is falling to pieces, break along with it. Trust that God will be what you need. Adjust your heart. Guide your steps. If you have had a bad report from a doctor or you are afraid for the health of someone you love, pray to Jesus, the one who healed the sick and performed miracles in the lives of everyday people.

When things get difficult, many run from God. Don't do that. Run to him. And don't fight the breaking. Forget trying to appear strong. Be weak. Be vulnerable. Be broken. It's in your weakness that you discover his strength. In your brokenness, you find his blessings.

> When things get difficult, many run from God. Don't do that. Run to him.

Let me remind you, this isn't advanced Christianity. Brokenness isn't just for monks and missionaries. Brokenness is actually the first step. It's basic Christianity. The gospel is an invitation to come and die. Die to your sins. Die to your past. Die to your flesh. And die to your fears.

It's not a comfortable, halfhearted, part-time commitment to Christ. It's a radical, daring submission to his will for your life.

You can play it safe. But my gut is you want more than that. I choose different. I am a faith-filled, bet-the-farm risk-taker. I will never insult God with small thinking or safe living. If there are blessings on the other side of brokenness, then break me.

When the sinful woman met the grace of Christ, she broke open her valuable bottle and poured out all the perfume.

When Jesus looked at those he loved and thought of those who were to come, he made a choice. He chose brokenness. His body was broken for you and his blood poured out for your sins.

> I will never insult God with small thinking or safe living.

Do you want more? Know there is more? Do you want to glorify God? Then go for it. Pray it. Step into it.

Live broken and poured out.

Are you ready?

It takes faith. It's not a safe prayer. There is no question it's dangerous.

But God's most intimate blessings await you on the other side.

"Lord, break me."

PART 3

SEND ME

Then I heard the Lord asking, "Whom should I send as a messenger to this people? Who will go for us?" I said, "Here I am. Send me."

—ISAIAH 6:8 NLT

SEND ME

As the son of a very patriotic dad, I learned how to salute our American flag at a young age. Not long after I began taking off my ball cap for the national anthem and placing my right hand over my heart, my father also told me a story about one of his favorite presidents. The streets of our capital were covered with eight inches of snow on that freezing cold day in January 1961. John F. Kennedy, the youngest man ever elected to our highest office, walked to the podium for his inauguration without wearing a coat or hat. Then, in a speech comprising less than fifteen hundred words and lasting less than fifteen minutes, President Kennedy delivered a famous challenge to future generations that still echoes today: "Ask not what your country can do for you. Ask what you can do for your country."

Even as a boy, every time I heard Dad describe that scene and say those words, I felt inspired. There was something so moving to me about JFK's challenge, an invitation to be part

107

of something bigger than myself, a plea to do more than to consume, but to contribute. Years later those few words still inspire me to serve my country, but they mean even more to me as I consider my prayer life before God.

Rather than asking God to serve *us*, what if we told God we are available to serve *him*?

As a pastor for several decades, I've seen firsthand the most intimate prayer requests of thousands of people. Each week, hundreds of needs flood our church, from prayer cards in our services to phone calls during the week or online requests through social media or our church app. So you won't be surprised to know the most common phrase I hear each week is one I'm delighted to fulfill: "Pastor, will you please pray for . . .?"

> Rather than asking God to serve *us*, what if we told God we are available to serve *him*?

I consider it a privilege, an honor, and a joyful responsibility to pause and lift up a need before the throne of God, asking him to have mercy, to move, to guide, to provide, to act, to do a miracle for people that I know and love. Each week someone asks that God would heal their loved one from cancer, help a neighbor find a job, or restore a hurting marriage. Students request prayer to get into the college of their choice, to help pay for that college, or to deal with the pain of their parents' divorce. Some people pray for a spouse. Others ask for help to forgive a person who hurt them. Some cry out for peace during a severe trial in life. Parents pray for teenagers succumbing to drugs. Men, and sometimes women, ask for help fighting addiction to porn. Both pray for healing from shame.

Even though the requests vary, people are asking God to do something for them or someone they love. God, help me. God, help someone I love. Lord, I need. Father, would you please.

God, do something for *me*.

Please hear me, we should definitely pray this way. We should always invite God's presence, God's power, God's peace to intervene in our lives. We should ask God to do miracles on our behalf. We should lift up our loved ones and remind ourselves of how God can move in their lives. We should seek the Lord for all of our needs.

But we shouldn't stop there.

In the spirit of JFK's inaugural address, what if we refused to just pray for ourselves? Forgive my paraphrase, but what if we prayed, "Ask not what God can do for you, but ask God what you can do for him?"

What if instead of asking God to just do something for us, we prayed a dangerous, self-denying prayer of availability to our heavenly Father?

> What if instead of always asking God to do something on our behalf, we dared to ask God to use us on his behalf?

What if instead of always asking God to do something on our behalf, we dared to ask God to use us on his behalf? What if we had the courageous faith to surrender our whole future—beginning right now—to God? Telling God we are all his.

Available. On call.

On standby to bless someone, serve someone, give all we can give to someone.

What if we prayed perhaps the most dangerous prayer of all?

"Send me, Lord. Use me."

WHEN GOD CALLS, ANSWER

When I tell you that "someone called me," you would probably assume a friend, relative, or church member punched in my cell number in hopes of talking to me or leaving a message (yes, you still can use your phone to make actual calls to other people—although they seem to be used for that purpose less and less). Long before phones, landlines, and mobiles, there was another kind of "call"—an invitation from God to serve him, usually in a specific, unique way. His call usually requires you to surrender your own plans and preferences and go where he tells you, when he tells you, how he tells you, to meet who he tells you, and to do what he tells you.

Complete surrender.

It's not easy to answer such a call, and we might be tempted to think of many excuses. We might even correctly think we're unqualified, inadequate, or unprepared to do what God asks us to do. But that's not a problem. You see, God never calls perfect people. God calls imperfect, flawed, weak men and women just like you and me. He simply wants people willing to be vessels, and he invites them to use their lives to make a difference for him.

Whenever I feel inadequate or unqualified, I remember that God called Moses, a murderer; David, an adulterer; and Rahab, a prostitute. Not only did God call people who did really bad things, but he also called unusual, insecure, and inconsistent people. Just consider some of God's chosen messengers, ministers, prophets, and leaders. There's Noah, who got drunk; Isaac, who was a daydreamer; Joseph, who was abandoned; and Gideon, who was afraid. There's Jeremiah, who was too young, and Abraham, who was too old. Elijah, who battled depression. Naomi, who became bitter. Martha, who was a worrywart. And John the Baptist, who ate bugs.

God never calls perfect people. God calls imperfect, flawed, weak men and women just like you and me.

Not exactly the Avengers, these folks. A far cry from any collection of super saints. But still God called them and used them even though they were far from perfect.

God hasn't changed. The same God who called imperfect people still does. Now he's calling you. Inviting you, nudging you, pulling you. God's call prompts you to live beyond yourself, to not just be about your own comfort but to completely surrender to his bidding. To go. To serve. To build. To love. To fight. To pray. To give. To lead.

So how do you respond when God calls you? In the Old Testament, we see at least three different responses. The prophet Jonah represents one of the most common responses: "Here I am, Lord, but I'm not going."

When the God of the universe saw a need in the city of Nineveh, he chose Jonah to go preach to the sinful and rebellious people there. Now Jonah had the gifts. He had the power. He had the ability. The problem is that he didn't have the availability. Jonah wasn't willing and flat-out told God, "No." And please understand, when God spoke, his assignment was clear: "Go to the great city of Nineveh and preach against it, because its wickedness has come up before me" (Jonah 1:2).

Jonah could have said, "Yes, anything for you, God. You are my Lord, and I will do what you ask." But that didn't happen. Instead of a willing heart, Jonah balked. He didn't just hesitate or make excuses; he ran away from God (see Jonah 1:3). And I have to wonder, did Jonah really think he could get far enough away? Or was it just a case of cultivating moment-by-moment denial to avoid the truth? Putting your head in the sand, or in Jonah's case, in the belly of a big fish. Trying to pretend—hoping— that God will just go away. Or change his mind about what he's called you to do.

Have you ever responded this way? Maybe you sensed God's prompting, an invitation to do something on his behalf. It might have been something small like giving a gift or sharing a thought. It might have been something more significant like changing careers or asking someone to marry you. But like Jonah, you hesitated. Stalled. Then turned the other way.

I know I've done this. One time I was driving home from work. My family lives only a short drive away from the city, but we still live close to thousands of acres of undeveloped land. It's not unusual to drive on backroads without seeing a single car or truck pass you. So driving home one day, I was shocked to see an older lady, in her midsixties or older, standing alone by the side of the road. No car nearby that might have broken down. Just this lady, standing there beside the ditch.

I was rattled. *What's she doing out here in the middle of nowhere? Is she lost? Looking for something? Waiting on someone? Just taking a stroll? Seems weird.* Everything inside me told me to stop. To check on her. To ask if she needed help. While I'm confident I felt God prompting me, I also knew it was common sense, just basic human decency to stop.

But I kept on driving.

Why didn't I stop? Why didn't I check on her? See if I could help? I've got absolutely no idea. I tried to rationalize it. *Surely she's fine. No one would be out on this road for no reason. She didn't wave me down or call out to me.*

But this moment of selfishness has haunted me ever since. Why didn't I stop? Why didn't I obey the prompting? Why didn't I offer assistance? For crying out loud, I'm a pastor. I'm supposed to be God's servant. His vessel. His hands and feet. But like Jonah, I took a selfish posture: "Here I am, Lord. I'm not going."

The second response to God's call may not be as outwardly rebellious, but it's just as dangerous to our spiritual health.

When God saw the oppressive power of Pharaoh to God's chosen people, he called Moses. God said, "So now, go. I am sending you to Pharaoh to bring my people the Israelites out of Egypt" (Ex. 3:10). Couldn't be clearer, right? God said, "I'm sending *you*. Now go! Out of all the people alive today, you're the one I selected. You're the one I called. You have what it takes. I'm sending you."

But Moses had a different response than Jonah. Instead of living in the confidence of God's calling, Moses was buried in his own insecurities. When God called his chosen vessel, Moses responded, "Who am I that I should go to Pharaoh and bring the Israelites out of Egypt?" (Ex. 3:11). Then Moses quickly told God all the reasons that he wasn't the right person. "I'm not a good speaker. I stutter. I'm not good enough. Someone else would be way better than me."

> Instead of living in the confidence of God's calling, Moses was buried in his own insecurities.

We still do this today. When God challenges us to give, we say, "But God, I don't have much for myself. Someone else can give more." When God calls us to serve, we might rationalize, "I don't have enough time. Surely there are better candidates for this role than me." When God prompts us to do something, we're tempted to tell him all the reasons we aren't his best person. We don't know enough. We aren't talented enough. We aren't good enough. There are so many others better qualified for this than us.

Here I am, God, but send someone else.

There is another response. And this one isn't just a statement to God, but it's a prayer. And as you probably guessed, it's dangerous. It's not a safe, benign, or self-centered prayer. This prayer requires great faith. It's risky because it will almost always move you to action. It will probably lead you to do something that may not seem natural or easy. It will cause you to step out of your comfort zone.

Isaiah prayed such a prayer of unreserved availability in the presence of God. The Old Testament prophet retells of his encounter with the Holy One when God asked, "Whom shall I send? And who will go for us?" (Isa. 6:8a) And without knowing the details, without knowing when or where, Isaiah prayed this stunning, life-altering prayer: "Here I am. Send me" (Isa. 6:8b NLT).

GLORY TO GOD

Let's be honest. Telling God you will do whatever he wants you to do is scary. Right? I remember talking to my friends about this kind of availability when I was in church youth group as a teenager. One of my buddies was convinced that God would send him to Africa as a missionary where he'd be broke, never see electricity again, and have to go to the bathroom in a hole in the ground. Another guy just knew he'd have to marry some Christian girl that he found unattractive. I remember thinking that if I prayed that dangerous prayer, God might make me become a pastor or something horrible like that. (How's that for a warning that this prayer is dangerous!)

How can you just do whatever God wants? He could ask you to do something you'd never want to do! Something overwhelming. Something unpleasant.

This type of dangerous prayer of submission is not easy to pray, especially if you don't have a deep trust and reverence for God. But when you do get to know God, his character, his nature, his holiness, you become more willing to offer this prayer. In fact, when you experience God for who he really is, you will actually enjoy praying with such vulnerability.

Isaiah didn't pray this prayer in a vacuum. It didn't come out of nowhere and for no reason. In the first verse of his book, Isaiah sets the context, explaining that his encounter with God took place in the year that King Uzziah died. Since Uzziah was a beloved and trusted king, Israel fell into a season of chaos, turmoil, and desperation without its popular leader. So it would have been logical for Isaiah to begin his prophecy with something dramatically ominous. He could have said, "In the lowest year of our nation . . ." Or he might have written, "In the year that we all lost hope . . ."

During this time of desperation and fear, however, Isaiah wrote, "In the year that King Uzziah died, I saw the Lord, high and exalted, seated on a throne; and the train of his robe filled the temple" (Isa. 6:1). Isaiah didn't just read about God or hear others talk about God. He *saw* the Lord. He experienced God's presence in a unique way. If you're going to ask God to use you, then a genuine encounter with him goes a long way in trusting him.

> If you're going to ask God to use you, then a genuine encounter with him goes a long way in trusting him.

You may sense God's presence while reading his Word. You may recognize that he is with you as you worship at church. You could find yourself overcome by his goodness while sitting on a mountaintop enjoying his creation. You may discover he is with you and gives you words to say when you are sharing your faith with a friend. Or you might feel all alone in a hard season of your life. But suddenly you become aware that you are not really alone. Not only is God with you in your pain, but he's always been there.

Isaiah saw the Lord. And in God's presence, Isaiah was stunned. He was shaken. He was astounded. God was high and lifted up. God was on his throne. The train of his robe filled the temple.

The prophet did his best to use human words to describe heavenly creatures encircling God, praising his name. Isaiah called them seraphim, angelic, fiery beings with six wings surrounding the Lord God. Because of the holiness of the Lord, these heavenly beings covered their faces with two of their wings to shield themselves from the glory of the Most High God. These worshipers cried out to each other with loud voices, shouting, "Holy, holy, holy is the LORD Almighty; the whole earth is full of his glory" (Isa. 6:3). Their voices boomed loud enough that the doorposts shook and the temple trembled. And the glory of God filled the temple.

When was the last time you had such an encounter with God that you were left in awe at his glory and holiness? Too often these days, many people treat him casually, even trivially. Familiar with popular perceptions of him but unaware of his holiness, many people take God for granted. To some, he's the "man upstairs" or the "big guy in the sky." But these pictures of God don't begin to come close to showing the Lord the respect, glory, and honor he deserves. If you ever caught a true vision of God in his purest essence, I promise you would never refer to him like a pal from down the road.

> If you ever caught a true vision of God in his purest essence, I promise you would never refer to him like a pal from down the road.

God is too mighty to disrespect. He is too holy to treat casually. He is too good to speak to with ungrateful familiarity. He is too majestic to casually take him for granted.

Let me give you a glimpse of who God is. Please read through his attributes slowly. Let them sink in. Let them amaze you. Let them overwhelm you. Be aware of what happens in your heart as you become even a bit more aware of his goodness, his grace, his glory. Get to know him more intimately. Embrace his holiness. Be in awe of his grandeur and glory.

Meditate on his character. Consider that God is the Creator of heaven and earth (Gen. 14:19). Scripture calls him God of glory (Ps. 29:3), the great I AM (Ex. 3:14), and righteous Father (John 17:25). God is our fortress of salvation (Ps. 28:8) and the eternal King (Jer. 10:10). He is the God of all comfort (2 Cor. 1:3), the God of all grace (1 Peter 5:10), and the God of peace (1 Thess. 5:23). He is the Almighty (Gen. 49:25), both compassionate and gracious (Ex. 34:6), and he is a consuming fire (Deut. 4:24).

I could go on—and it might draw you closer into his

presence to seek out and meditate on other attributes of God. I find it helpful to personalize the presence and attributes of God. He's not just our God, but he's also *my* God. If you know Christ—if you have committed your life to following him as a disciple—he is your God too.

Feel the power of his presence. If his Spirit dwells within you, you can say with confidence: He is my Rock (Ps. 42:9). He is my Savior (Ps. 18:46). He is my stronghold (Ps. 144:2). My God is the one who blots out our sins (Isa. 43:25), and he is my God who comforts me when I hurt (Isa. 66:13). The King of the universe is my advocate (Job 16:19). He is my comforter in sorrow (Jer. 8:18). He is my confidence when I'm unsure (Ps. 71:5). He is my strength when I'm weak (2 Cor. 12:10). God is my helper (Ps. 118:7), my hiding place (Ps. 32:7), my hope (Ps. 25:5, 21), my light (Ps. 27:1). He is my refuge in time of trouble (Ps. 59:16), he is my song (Ex. 15:2 NLT), and he is my strong deliverer (Ps. 140:7).

God is holy—set apart and perfect in all his glory.

So holy is God that he cannot look upon sin (Hab. 1:13).

So holy is God that mortal man cannot look upon him in his purest essence and live (Ex. 33:20).

And this holy, otherworldly God is slow to anger and abounding in love (Ex. 34:6). Not just for humankind, but for you.

When you become aware of his presence, you will not be the same.

Some might push back, saying, "Okay, Craig. I get it. If I saw God like Isaiah did, I might be willing to pray that dangerous prayer too. But I've never experienced the presence of God like that. My time with the Lord doesn't have that kind of drama." Well, let me encourage you to rethink your time with God. Not only is it possible to experience him like Isaiah experienced him, but God wants to reveal himself to you.

James, the half brother of Jesus, instructs us to draw close to God and promises that God will meet us when we do. James said, "Come near to God and he will come near to you" (James 4:8). In the Old Testament, God was talking about prayer, explaining that he listens when his people pray. Then God boldly promises his children that you will find him when you seek him with your whole heart (see Jer. 29:13).

God is not playing hide and seek. He wants you to know him and delights in showing himself to you. Seek him. Draw near to him. Cry out to him. He is there.

> God is not playing hide and seek. He wants you to know him and delights in showing himself to you.

You will experience him when you seek him, watch for him, and cry out to him. You might feel his presence as you drive down the road singing along to a worship song. You might sense his presence as you sit in awe of his creation, admiring his work as the sun rises brilliantly in the morning. You might notice that he is with you during a simple bedtime prayer with your child. The doorposts don't have to shake to know he is with you. It may be a simple awareness that he never leaves you and will never forsake you.

You may feel his presence in a supernatural way. You may know that he is with you. But even if you don't feel him, you can rest assured that he is with you. Sometimes you know he is with you, not by feeling, but by faith. How do you grow toward not only praying but living this dangerous prayer?

It starts with experiencing God's presence.

A SINNER SAVED BY GRACE

When I was a kid, I wanted to feel God's presence. Especially in church—after all, that's God's house, right?—I expected to feel something supernatural, for lack of a better word. Goosebumps would have been cool. A tingle down my spine would have been great. I could imagine his peace and comfort as this heavenly warmth radiated inside me. But it never happened. Mostly I just felt uncomfortable in the dress clothes my parents made me wear to church and wondered how much longer until we could leave and have lunch.

While all these feelings are possible, I've found that encounters with God are usually more than tingles in your body or the warmth you feel when holding a puppy. But before we can encounter God, it often helps to deal with the sin in our lives. To truly get to a point of submission and availability to God, and to be fully aware of his presence, we are wise to recognize and understand our sinfulness.

Just to say that we're "sinners" offends so many people today. In our culture, there are self-help gurus and motivational experts who tell us to reject the idea that we're sinful. We should just love ourselves the way we are. No need to change unless we want to change—and then we can do it ourselves.

> To truly get to a point of submission and availability to God, and to be fully aware of his presence, we are wise to recognize and understand our sinfulness.

In fact, I was talking to a guy at the gym recently who was telling me that he didn't need Jesus in his life. With complete confidence, he told me that even though Jesus was probably a real person and maybe even the Son of God, Jesus was useless to him. When I asked him if he ever had any need of forgiveness, the man responded strongly, "Absolutely not." He explained that he was a "good person" and way better than many Christians he knew. Why would he need to be forgiven if he wasn't bad?

Although I'm certain this guy did many good things, I tried to help him recognize that at our core, none of us are good. Because of the rebellion all the way back in the garden of Eden, we inherited what is called the *sin nature* of Adam. The apostle Paul explained it this way: "Just as sin entered the world through one man, and death through sin, and in this way death came to all people, because all sinned" (Rom. 5:12).

When we see how good God is, we become acutely aware of how good we are *not*. His holiness reveals our sinfulness. This is what happened to Isaiah, and this is what happens to us in God's presence. When the prophet saw the glory of God, he didn't cry out, "I am amazing. I'm holy and perfect like God." No, Isaiah recognized the depths of his own depravity and shouted, "Woe to me! . . . I am ruined! For I am a man of unclean lips, and I live among a people of unclean lips, and my eyes have seen the King, the LORD Almighty" (Isa. 6:5).

Isaiah didn't just say, "I messed up. I did a few bad things." He cried from a heart of despair, "Woe to me!" The awareness of the depths of his sin brought sadness, remorse, grief, and a spirit of sincere repentance. In God's presence, Isaiah said, "I'm ruined." Another version translates the original Hebrew text as "I'm undone."

In a similar response, Moses hid his face, because he was afraid to look upon God (Ex. 3:6). Job said he despised or abhorred himself when he saw the power of God (Job 42:6). Peter fell facedown at the Lord's feet and told Jesus to depart from him because of his sinfulness (Luke 5:8). None of us are any better than Moses, Job, or Peter. And some of us even had similar experiences when we prayed to God for salvation. Even if you didn't fall facedown, giving your life to Jesus begins with an awareness of your need for salvation from sin.

But why do we need to recognize our sin? Can't we just start following Jesus and move on? What's the big deal about looking at how selfish and rebellious we are? Because until we see ourselves as sinners, we'll never fully understand Jesus as the Savior.

Like my friend at the gym, for years, I too tried to rationalize my own sinfulness, even after I became a follower of God.

After all, I knew people who were way worse than I was. I never murdered anyone. I wasn't a gang member or an abuser. But when I started praying dangerously—crying out to God and getting to know who he was—my self-confidence grew into self-awareness. God is righteous. I'm unrighteous. God is full of glory. I'm full of myself. I had to face the brutal truth about my sinfulness. I was selfish. I often told lies, and occasionally I took things that were not mine. I envied others, lusted, and wanted the shiny things this world offered.

But when you pray dangerous prayers, you will see and understand more of God. It changes everything. Isaiah saw it. Maybe you will too. When the angelic beings sang of the holiness of God, Isaiah knew his own lips were sinful and unclean. We will see our sinfulness in full only when we embrace God's holiness. As long as we compare ourselves with other people, we can deceive ourselves that we are not that bad. But when we compare ourselves to God, we see just how unrighteous we truly are. Like Isaiah, as I experienced the presence of God, I became aware of my sin. This awareness then led me to a fuller understanding of God's amazing grace.

> When you pray dangerous prayers, you will see and understand more of God. It changes everything.

One of my strongest seasons of spiritual growth came when I was a young associate pastor at First United Methodist Church in Oklahoma City. As hard as it is to admit, in so many ways, I was "playing a part" more than I was "living a calling."

Feeling the pressure to live up to high expectations, I started to say things that sounded "pastoral," even if they weren't completely true. I'd tell people that I'd be praying for them, even if I knew that I probably wouldn't. I'd act like I was close to God, even though I was over my head with work and hadn't spent much time with God at all.

One Thursday morning, while I was preparing to preach in the place of my senior pastor, I felt like God opened my eyes to my sinfulness. The image God gave me was clear: I'd become a "full-time pastor" and a "part-time follower of Christ." I was showing an outward life that wasn't a true reflection of inward devotion. So in one of my more dangerous faith moves, I scrapped the sermon that I was preparing and preached a more authentic message from my heart confessing how I'd drifted from God. To this day, I don't know if I remember God doing more in the lives of so many people than he did on the day I bared my soul before our church family.

At the depths of Isaiah's despair, he experienced the deepness of God's grace. He tried to put words to what happened when one of the fiery seraphim flew in his direction. The angelic being carried a burning, red-hot coal that he had removed straight from the altar of God. When the creature touched the flaming coal to the prophet's lips, God's messenger said, "See, this has touched your lips; your guilt is taken away and your sin atoned for" (Isa. 6:7).

Imagine the power of the moment. Isaiah has never been more aware of his guilt, his sin, his shame. And with one touch from God's being, his sin was gone. Forgotten. Forgiven. First, unconditional grace. Then, uncontainable gratitude.

My sins are forgiven.

There is nothing better to fuel your prayer life than a deep appreciation for God's grace. Imagine God wiping away all your lies. Healing your hatred. Cleansing your sexual sin.

Embrace it. If you are "in Christ," your self-centered decisions are forgiven. Your anger—forgiven. Hatred—forgiven. Bitterness—forgiven. Boasting—forgiven. Jealousy—forgiven. Envy—forgiven. All your sins, your evil thoughts, your greed, your hypocrisy, your filthy gossip, your secret lusts, your pride, your ingratitude, your materialism, your unbelief—all forgiven and forgotten by the grace of our good God.

Later in his life, Isaiah would add color to God's grace by quoting the one who forgave him, writing, "I, even I, am he who blots out your transgressions, for my own sake, and remembers your sins no more" (Isa. 43:25). When you cry out to God for forgiveness, he doesn't remember your sins. They are gone. Forgiven. Washed away. And forgotten.

In the same way that the coal removed Isaiah's guilt and sin, the blood of Jesus takes away ours. As you read, I hope you will pause long enough to let these truths sink in, soothe your sin-stained soul, and inspire you to pray dangerous prayers.

Grace. Changes. Everything.

We don't bring anything.

Jesus brings everything.

When we sense his presence, we become aware of our

sinfulness. Then we become eternally indebted to him for his extravagant, undeserved, and matchless grace.

The moment we see God for who he is, we see ourselves for what we are not. And because of what Jesus did for us and the grace he lavishes on us, suddenly the dangerous prayer of surrender doesn't seem so daunting.

In fact, though still dangerous, it might feel somewhat inviting. When God asks, "Who will go? Whom shall I send?" our immediate response from a forgiven and surrendered heart is the faith-filled, fully available prayer: "Here I am, Lord. Send me."

> The moment we see God for who he is, we see ourselves for what we are not.

And when you pray this dangerous prayer, it's not out of obligation or guilt. *You know, because of what Jesus did for me and all, I've got to be available to him now, I guess.* No, it's a daring prayer of faith. It's the deep realization that your life is not your own. You belong to God. You are his servant. His ambassador. His representative on earth.

Your prayers will start to grow from self-focused requests— "Do this for me, God. Help me, Lord"—into Christ-centered, gospel-powered, God-glorifying prayers. "Anywhere, God. Anytime. Whatever you want, I'm yours."

You recognize that the same God who has forgiven you has also called you and chosen you. Every single day, he has appointments planned for you. People to bless. Things to give. Opportunities to serve.

When you are surrendered to him, you will have eyes to

see where he's working. A heart to feel what touches his heart. And hands to show his love.

You will see people who need encouragement, and his Spirit will give you words to say. You will see someone who has a need, and God will prompt you to meet the need. You will see someone who is alone, and you will show them God's love. You are his servant. Available. Eager. And ready to go.

When you are surrendered to him, you will have eyes to see where he's working. A heart to feel what touches his heart. And hands to show his love.

DAILY NOURISHMENT

But before you think you can pray "send me" and be done, let me warn you: this isn't a one-time dangerous prayer you pray and then you go on with your life. This is another prayer of daily submission to God. *Search me. Break me. Send me.*

Why are these *daily* prayers? Because when you submit your life to Christ, your spirit comes to life. You are born anew, and your spirit is connected to God's Spirit. From that moment on, there is a war going on within you.

Paul calls it a battle between your flesh and your spirit. By flesh, he's not talking about your skin. Paul is referring to our sinful nature. Your old nature wants to do what's easiest for you. Your new and spiritual nature wants to do what glorifies God. And those two natures square off against each other multiple times a day for as long as you live. Paul described this to the Galatians, saying, "For the flesh desires what is contrary to the Spirit, and the Spirit what is contrary to the flesh. They are in conflict with each other, so that you are not to do whatever you want" (Gal. 5:17). The Holy Spirit inside you says, "Live for God." Your flesh says, "Live for yourself." When God calls, the part of you that is selfish says, like Jonah, "I'm not going." Or like Moses, "Send someone else."

How do we live submitted to God when our flesh wants us living for ourselves? How do we overcome our selfish tendencies and live selflessly for Christ? The answer lies in daily submission. Daily we should feed our spirits. Because what we feed grows. You know that's true. If you fertilize your houseplants and water them, they will grow. If you feed your cat too much, your cat will be fat. If you feed your ego, your ego will grow. What you feed grows.

And what you starve dies.

If you don't feed and water your houseplants, they will wilt. If you don't feed your cat, your cat's future is not bright. If you starve someone from affection, they die slowly on the inside.

What you feed grows. What you starve dies.

What you feed grows. What you starve dies.

So feed your spirit daily. Give it nourishment by reading the Bible. Spend time in God's presence by praying. Enjoy God's goodness by engaging in fellowship with other believers. Hear God's voice by reading the Bible.

And starve your sinful self. Rather than getting what you want, give up something you may want, for something you want even more—a God-glorifying life. Deny the desires of your flesh, saying no to what you know is less than God's best. Run away from something that would tempt you to do wrong.

This is exactly what happened to my close friend "Travis." When Travis was in junior high, he found his dad's hidden stash of *Playboy* magazines. Like most curious thirteen-year-olds with very little restraint, his curiosity got the best of him. What started out as a quick peek grew into an out-of-control addiction that followed him into adulthood and marriage. When I asked him about his secret viewing habits, he brushed me off like I was some old-fashioned prude. "Every guy looks," he told me, followed with his strongest justification: "At least I'm not doing something worse."

For years, Travis struggled in his marriage and rationalized his porn addiction. Since Travis hated to read, he rarely cracked open his Bible. But when our church created the YouVersion Bible app, an app that you don't just read but will also read to you aloud, he no longer had an excuse.

Travis started listening to different Bible plans. And he told me that almost every one that he chose mentioned something about lust, purity, or the dangers of fulfilling the desires of the flesh. Travis was ready to admit that perhaps he had a problem.

When he tried to quit his daily doses of adrenaline-infused visual entertainment, he discovered that he was more trapped than he realized. After confessing his problem to his wife, he joined a support group for sex addicts, and they quickly pointed him to God's power-packed promise of freedom. The apostle Paul declared boldly, "No temptation has overtaken you except what is common to mankind. And God is faithful; he will not let you be tempted beyond what you can bear. But when you are tempted, he will also provide a way out so that you can endure it" (1 Cor. 10:13). That's all Travis needed. He memorized that verse. He declared it daily. He put a tracking device on his computer, canceled his cable channels, and put strict locks on his phone. With the help of God's Word, a praying wife, and good friends, Travis has been porn-free for over four years. And it started with God's Word giving him the strength to overcome.

When you start to avoid what hurts you, what happens? Over time, your spiritual side grows stronger. And your selfish side starts to die.

Your prayers will deepen, mature, and grow. Instead of just, "Bless me. Help me. Do this for me," your prayers become God-centered and others-focused. "God, use me to be a voice of encouragement today. Give me a chance to help someone who is in need. Help me show your love to someone who is hurting. If I have anything that would help someone, show me how to bless them. Here I am. Send me."

> When you start to avoid what hurts you, what happens? Over time, your spiritual side grows stronger. And your selfish side starts to die.

When you become available to God, he might ask you to go to Africa as a missionary, but it's far more likely he will invite you to be a missionary at your work. Chances are good that he will prompt you to show those you interact with daily his love, his grace. When you pray a dangerous prayer of submission, God may ask you to sell everything and give it to the poor. It's far more likely that he will start to move you to manage wisely what he's given you. To tithe to your church. To give to those who are in need. And to make a difference a little at a time.

When you become available to God, he might ask you to go to Africa as a missionary, but it's far more likely he will invite you to be a missionary at your work.

When you fully submit to God, he will certainly ask you to do things that may seem simple and small. You may even wonder, *Why don't I get to do something big, something important?* And God may show you that the small things are often the big things. The simple acts of love often lead to the biggest changes in life.

And as you grow in your trust in God, every now and then, he will ask you to do something radical. Something that doesn't make any sense. Something that takes extraordinary faith. God may lead you to move to a new city. To start a new ministry. To launch a business. To foster or to adopt. God may prompt you to go to another part of the world to serve someone. Or to give an extravagant gift to someone in need.

Even though it may seem crazy, irrational, and like it makes no sense at all, you will have the faith to say yes. Because you understand, your life is his.

When God uses you, you will want more. More fulfillment. More joy you find in sacrifices. More blessings that come from obedience. You can live in the daily thrill of being used by God. A reflection of his grace and glory. A conduit of his love and goodness.

But only if you're willing.

A SINGLE ACT OF FAITH

Years ago, I finally started journaling consistently. The reason I say "finally" is because I must have tried to journal four or five different times, only to quit each time after a few weeks. Someone got Amy and me a journal that we loved to use. It's a five-year journal that has only five or six lines to write on daily. If it happens to be July 28th, we can see just above the day what happened on July 28th the year before and the year before that. The highlights of five years of our lives are stacked on top of each other on a single given page.

As I journaled, I started to notice that many of my days were similar. Last year on the same day, I was doing the same thing. Most days, I do the same things. I go to meetings. Study. Preach sermons. Work out. Have family dinners. Although I did have the joy of being used by God as a pastor, so much of that is a result of my "job," not just regular faith in following Christ.

During one of my dangerous prayers of submission, God prompted me to add one small thing to my life that has made a big difference. Since we cannot please God without faith (see Heb. 11:6), I believe God asked me to simply do one thing daily that takes faith. Every day, no matter what, at least one faith-filled act.

That simple challenge changed the way I lived. Instead of existing passively, I started living aggressively, watching for opportunities to exhibit faith. When I met a guy that seemed discouraged on a flight, I talked to him and did my best to lift his spirits. Then I felt prompted by God to do more than just talk. I wrote him a note and included two different verses from the Bible. Rather than just hearing encouragement, I wanted him to have a recorded version that he could revisit.

> Instead of existing passively, start living aggressively, watching for opportunities to exhibit faith.

Another time, when Amy and I were in the grocery store shopping, we saw a woman with three children meticulously examining the prices, sorting coupons, and adding the amounts on her phone calculator. Knowing she was obviously strapped financially, as an act of faith, we had one of our children take her some cash with a note that simply said, "God cares about you and wants to meet your needs." We don't know how God used that in her life, but believing that he did changed us.

Here's another example. Recently I landed in Florida for an event. The host, a successful businessman in the area, picked me up at the airport and immediately put me at ease. His love for Jesus was obvious and his heart to serve was strong. Even though he excelled as an entrepreneur, I suddenly had a sense that he might be called by God to use his gifts in ministry. So I took a small step of faith and asked him, "Have you ever considered using your talents full time for God?" He almost wrecked the car as he told me that he had just mentioned that to his wife the night before! Now he's giving serious consideration to selling his business to pursue something different.

At first, doing something daily that takes faith may seem daunting or even overwhelming. But once you start, not only will you enjoy it, but you may even sense God transforming you from someone with a self-centered faith to someone with a self-sacrificing, God-glorifying, other-centered faith. Your faith acts don't have to be big, intimidating, or newsworthy. They can be simple, unassuming, and even performed in secret.

It's simply a matter of being willing, being open, being attuned to God, and risking more. Take the focus off yourself and notice the needs of others. Listen with your heart and not just your ears. Read between the lines and look for a way to serve.

> Your faith acts don't have to be big, intimidating, or newsworthy. They can be simple, unassuming, and even performed in secret.

What if you told God you were available? And you looked for at least one opportunity daily to do something that required faith? Instead of living a *meh* life, small acts of faith teach us to depend on God. They draw us close to him. They build our trust.

Pray just one dangerous prayer.

Risk just one act of faith.

YOUR WILL BE DONE

Not long after I began taking at least one faith risk each day, I also expanded the way I pray for God to use me. Instead of simply asking God to send me, I personalized it. Since God created every part of my body, I take time to pause, pray, and devote specific parts of my body to him. This short prayer to God energizes me spiritually, it empowers me emotionally, and it emboldens me to do his will. My dangerous prayer of dedication varies slightly each day, but it generally goes something like this:

> Heavenly Father, because you gave Jesus for me, I give my whole day to you today. Every part of me is yours. Take each part of the body you created and consecrate it for your purposes today.
>
> God, I give you my mind. Please guard my thoughts. Help me take captive any thought that is not from you to

God, I give you my mind. Please guard my thoughts. Help me take captive any thought that is not from you to make it obedient to Christ and all your truth. make it obedient to Christ and all your truth. Renew my mind. May all my thoughts be pleasing to you. Help me to think on things that are pure, excellent, and worthy of praise. Help me to think your thoughts. Direct my mind toward your perfect will today.

Lord, I give you my eyes. Help me to look on things that are pure and honoring to you. Protect my eyes from lusting after the temporary pleasures of this world. Give me eyes to see what you see. Since my eyes are the lamp of my body, help me see things that let your light shine through my life today.

God, guard my ears. Protect me from listening to any lies from the evil one. May I only hear your voice, your Spirit, your truth guiding me. Lord, help me turn from any voice that distracts me from your plan for my life today. May I be sensitive to everything you say to me. Interrupt my plans. Redirect me toward your agenda. Give me ears to hear your voice so I may follow where you lead.

God, set a guard over my mouth. May every word that I speak be pleasing to you, O God. Give me words to say to lift and encourage others, pointing them to you. I know my words have the power to give life and to take life. Empower me to speak life to everyone that I see.

Lord, help me guard my heart, as I know it can easily deceive me. Purify my motives in all that I do. May my only goal be to serve and please you. God, help my heart be moved by what moves your heart, be broken by what breaks yours, and rejoice in the things that bring you joy. Create in me a clean heart, God. Help me to love and serve you today with my whole heart.

———————

God, may my hands be your hands in the world today. I devote the work of my hands to you. Empower me to be productive today, honoring you in all the work that I do. Help me, God, to do everything for your glory.

Lord, direct the steps of my feet. May your Word be a lamp directing all my steps. Guide me to the right places and right people so I can serve you best today. Keep me from the wrong places that might tempt me to sin against you. Guide my feet, Lord, into your perfect will.

God, my whole body is yours. I know that before I was even created, you had good works, prepared in advance, for me to do today. Use me, God, to do them all. You have given me everything I need to do everything you have called me to do. Help me to see needs and meet them. Show me those who are hurting that I could encourage them. Direct me to

Lord, help me guard my heart, as I know it can easily deceive me. Purify my motives in all that I do. May my only goal be to serve and please you.

those without you so I could help them know your goodness and grace.

God, I devote every part of me to you and to your will today.

Here I am, Lord. Send me.

Most days, I pray some version of this dangerous prayer. You don't have to pray these words, but I hope you'll consider surrendering more of yourself to God each day. Pray what's on your heart and give yourself to be used by God. Invite him to send you into opportunities where you can be salt and light and see what happens—in you and in those around you.

Make the words of your prayer your own. My words change slightly, but my intention behind them always remains the same: "God, may your will be done through me today." It shouldn't be surprising to me, but when I don't take time to pray this prayer, my days are not as productive. I'm often more distracted, more self-focused, more easily tempted. But when I do pray this prayer, my heart stays directed toward what matters to God. I am more aware of the gentle, soft promptings of the Holy Spirit guiding me to say something to a coworker or to help a friend. When I start my day wholly devoted to God, my mind is focused toward what lasts rather than the temporary pleasures of this world. My day matters to God. And it's meaningful to me.

And at the end of the day, I can look back and see all the different ways that God used me. As I write in my journal, I can note how I took steps of faith. And rather than feeling empty, hollow, and dissatisfied, I feel fulfilled, content, and overwhelmed with gratitude toward God.

How do you think your life might change if you prayed daily a daring, faith-filled prayer of whole-life devotion to the one who gave it all for you?

What if right now you prayed, "Send me, Lord"?

> How do you think your life might change if you prayed daily a daring, faith-filled prayer of whole-life devotion to the one who gave it all for you?

NOW WHAT'S THE QUESTION?

Years ago, I heard a pastor tell a story that I'll never forget. This seasoned preacher described how each week, after the Sunday service, he'd stand by the door of the church to greet people as they left for their cars. He described the joy of hugging the grandmas and high-fiving the younger kids week after week. The pastor admitted openly that he loved when his parishioners would praise his message, complimenting him on how God used him to speak to them.

But then the pastor described an encounter he had with a guy, Matt, that he'd seen regularly at church but had never gotten to know well. Matt was probably in his midforties, graying slightly around the temples. Lines around his eyes indicated he might have had some challenging years in his life, but his warm smile and confident handshake led the preacher to believe that Matt was probably in a better season in life at the moment.

Then one Sunday after the service, Matt grasped both of

the pastor's hands firmly and said, "Pastor, I want you to know that my answer is yes. Now what's the question?"

The pastor looked at Matt curiously. *Poor guy, what's he talking about? The answer is yes? What does that mean?* Not wanting to make it awkward, the pastor grinned at the man, nodded, and said, "Thank you, Matt. God bless you."

The next Sunday after church, Matt approached the pastor at the door and said the exact same thing. With heartfelt sincerity, he looked the pastor directly in the eyes and said, "Pastor, I want you to know that my answer to you will always be yes. Now what's the question?"

The pastor assumed he wasn't hearing Matt correctly. It just didn't make sense. Once again, he nodded and shook Matt's hand and kept the line moving.

The following Sunday, it happened again. This time the pastor knew that he'd heard Matt correctly. But the pastor was still confused. *What does he mean by that? The answer is yes—the answer to what?*

Not wanting to stop the greeting line for a longer conversation, he asked Matt if they could visit later over coffee. Matt smiled broadly and handed the pastor his business card for his contact information. "Of course we can have coffee! I told you my answer is yes."

On Tuesday that week, the two men met at the coffee shop. After finishing the obligatory small talk, the pastor leaned in slightly and said, "I've been wondering about what you said to me. What do you mean the answer is yes?"

Matt leaned back with a look of deep satisfaction, as if he'd been waiting his whole life for the pastor to ask him that question.

He started talking slowly, carefully choosing his words. "I was not always the man that I am today. I did a lot of bad things in my life, hurt a lot of people. I was addicted to alcohol, pornography, and gambling. Those addictions ruled my life. I betrayed my wife, crushed my children, caused so much pain." Matt choked up, and the pastor could see tears forming in the man's eyes.

Assuming they were tears of pain and regret, the pastor was startled to hear Matt say, "But I'm thankful now for those low times. Because that's what helped me to be open to Christ. You see, when I hit bottom, a friend invited me to church. And that's when I heard you preach about the grace of Christ."

When the man said the word *Christ*, the tears started to flow. Matt continued telling his story without even trying to hide his obvious emotion. "At first, I just listened, not sure if I could believe it was true for me. But after a few months, I invited Christ into my life and he changed me."

At that point, the pastor couldn't keep his own tears back. The two men sat there silently for a moment. Both changed by the same Savior. Both grateful for the brief, holy moment they shared together over a cup of coffee.

Then the man said, "Pastor, that's why I want you to know my answer to you is always yes. Because of how Jesus changed my life through our church, I will always be available to him—and to you. If you ask me to mow the church yard, I will be honored to do it. If you need money to help a single mom, I will give without hesitation. If you need someone to drive a widow to church, I'm your driver. Pastor, I want you to know that my answer is yes. So just let me know the question."

Now that's the heart of a person that God can use.

Such openness is the essence of this dangerous prayer. When Isaiah experienced the presence of God, he became aware of his own sinful brokenness. Then the seraph touched his lips with the flaming coal and God forgave his sin. Because of God's goodness, God's grace, and God's love, Isaiah's response was bold. Send me. Anywhere. Anytime. I will sign my name to a blank contract of availability. God, you just fill in the details.

Use me. My life is completely yours. May your will become my will. Your plan, my plan.

> Because of who you are—my God, my King, my Savior, I trust you. Because you are sovereign over the universe, I surrender my will to you, every part of me.

Notice Isaiah didn't ask for any details. He didn't ask God where. Or when. Or what would happen. This is why this prayer can feel so dangerous. "God, send me. Use me. I'm not asking for details. I don't need to know the benefits. Or if it will be easy. Or if I will enjoy it. Because of who you are—my God, my King, my Savior—I trust you. Because you are sovereign over the universe, I surrender my will to you, every part of me. Take my mind, my eyes, my mouth, my ears, my heart, my hands, and my feet and guide me toward your will. I trust you. God, my answer is yes. Now what's the question?"

Imagine if you prayed this way. Are you sick of safe prayers? Are you tired of living for things that don't matter? Do you despise halfhearted, lukewarm Christianity? Then pray the dangerous prayer.

Do you despise halfhearted, lukewarm Christianity? Then pray the dangerous prayer.

Here I am, Lord.

Send me.

Use me.

DISTURB ME, LORD

*I love the L*ORD *because he hears my voice and my prayer for mercy. Because he bends down to listen, I will pray as long as I have breath!*

—PSALM 116:1–2 NLT

What we pray about is important. But not only is it important, it's also revealing.

The content of our prayers tells us more about us and our relationship with God than most people might imagine. What we pray for reflects what we believe about God. If most of our prayers are for "ourselves" or "what matters to us," then the content of our prayers communicates that we believe, deep down, that God exists primarily for *us*.

So take a moment and do a prayer audit. Think about

everything you prayed for recently—not your whole lifetime, just the past seven days. Consider writing on a notepad or typing a memo on your phone and listing all the different things you petitioned God to do in the last week. Take a moment and give it some thought. Do you remember? What did you pray about? What did you ask God to do?

Now answer honestly. If God said yes to every prayer you prayed in the last seven days, how would the world be different?

> Answer honestly. If God said yes to every prayer you prayed in the last seven days, how would the world be different?

If your prayers were the normal, safe ones, then maybe you would have had a good day, arrived safely, or enjoyed a blessed double cheeseburger, fries, and Diet Coke.

Or if you ventured out into slightly bigger prayers, maybe you would have nailed a presentation at work, or landed a new client, even though you were really unprepared. Maybe you would have gotten that front-row parking spot you asked God for in the busy parking lot at the mall. Or maybe, just maybe, you would have won the lottery.

For years, if I did a prayer audit, the results would have been dismal. If God had done everything over a week's period that I had asked him to do, the world wouldn't have been much different at all. Honestly, some weeks I wouldn't have prayed for anything. Other weeks, I might have prayed, but the prayers were all about me, and that doesn't change much in the grand scheme of things.

My prayers were too safe.

I had access to the Creator and Sustainer of the universe. The Great I AM. The Alpha and the Omega. The Beginning and the End. The all-powerful, ever-present, all-knowing God who can send fire from heaven, shut the mouths of hungry lions, or calm a raging storm. And all I asked him to do was keep me safe and help me have a good day.

Then one day I came across a prayer attributed to Sir Francis Drake, an English sea captain who lived from 1540–96. His prayer messed me up. It wasn't easy to pray. And it definitely wasn't safe. This dangerous prayer helped stretch me, to move me from comfortably coasting to soaring by faith. As our time together comes to a close, I encourage you to take a few minutes and read through Drake's words slowly.

Disturb us, Lord, when we are too well pleased with ourselves, when our dreams have come true because we have dreamed too little, when we arrived safely because we sailed too close to the shore.

Disturb us, Lord, when with the abundance of things we possess, we have lost our thirst for the waters of life; having fallen in love with life, we have ceased to dream of eternity, and in our efforts to build a new earth, we have allowed our vision of the new heaven to dim.

Disturb us, Lord, to dare more boldly, to venture on wider seas, where storms will show your mastery; where losing sight of land, we shall find the stars. We ask you to push back the horizon of our hopes; and to push back the future in strength, courage, hope, and love.

This we ask in the name of our Captain, who is Jesus Christ.

Amen!*

And that's what God did. He disturbed me.

For years, I never wanted to be interrupted. But after praying more dangerous prayers, I discovered that God's gentle promptings would regularly interrupt my self-centered plans and he would direct me toward his eternal will. Instead of being limited by what I wanted, God helped me to care more about others and consider what he wants. Instead of craving a life of comfort, I've found joy in serving the needs of others through daily acts of faith. Rather than trying to control my life, I've learned to trust God moment by moment, even if he breaks me. I'm far from perfect—some would say I'm more disturbed than ever—but I'm closer to God.

> Instead of craving a life of comfort, I've found joy in serving the needs of others through daily acts of faith.

My faith is stronger.

My life is richer.

Prayers for a Pilgrim Church Blog, "Disturb Us, Lord—A Prayer of Sir Francis Drake," blog entry by Danut Manastireanu, January 13, 2016, https://pilgrimchurchprayers.wordpress.com/2016/01/13/disturb-us-lord-a-prayer-of-sir-francis-drake/.

My heart is fuller.

I believe God wants to disturb you too. And if you've made it to the end of this book, then you must be craving more from your relationship with God. You long to know him, talk to him, listen to him, and be guided by him. You hunger to make a difference. You ache to glorify God with how you live your life.

It's time to change the way you pray.

It's time to seek God passionately, with every fiber of your being. It's time to abandon safe, comfortable, predictable, and easy-to-pray prayers. It's time to pray with courage, to risk, to open yourself up to a different path to a better destination. It's time to start praying dangerous prayers.

> It's time to pray with courage, to risk, to open yourself up to a different path to a better destination.

It's time to be disturbed.

Think about what could be different if you prayed with more transparency. If you risked more. If you were more open to what God might do in you instead of just hoping he will do something for you. What if you prayed bolder prayers? Dreamed bigger? Recklessly pursued Jesus with daring, self-abandoned faith?

Have the courage to ask God to search you. Give him permission to know your heart, to see if you have anything offensive dwelling in your soul. To lead you to his plan. When you do, maybe God will reveal a corner of darkness in your heart and transform it with his glorious light. And you will never be the same again.

Or do you dare pray for God to break you? It's scary, no doubt. You may not hear from him right away. Then one day, he will answer that dangerous prayer. And the breaking will be more painful than you could imagine. But so is the intimacy, the strength of his presence, and the unwavering confidence in the goodness of God on the other side of your pain. You won't want to go through the breaking again. But you would also never change what God did in you through your brokenness.

You will be different. Your faith will be deeper.

You are his. He is yours (Ps. 100:3).

Once you know God so well, you won't want to wait for him to send you. To use you for his purposes to serve and to love, to minister and to give, to forgive and to heal. Sent by God, you may confront some injustice, right some wrong, meet some need. He will be glorified. The lives and hearts of other men and women will be changed. And you will know that you obeyed God and showed his love.

Instead of being obsessed with comfort, you will live for a calling. God will stretch you out of your comfort zone and you will lead people to know Jesus. One day, perhaps, God will hear your faith-filled cries in heaven and heal someone from cancer on earth. Perhaps as you are speaking to God, he will speak to you. Maybe he will nudge you out of your comfort zone and you will have your first serious discussion about adopting a child. Or you will obey the voice of God and pay for someone's groceries. Or you will follow the prompting of God's Spirit and commit to go on your church's upcoming mission trip.

No matter what, your life won't stay the same. When you pray dangerously, your life simply *can't* remain the same.

If you truly want to make a difference on earth, you need power from heaven. If you want your life to matter, it's time to pray big, bold, audacious prayers.

> When you pray dangerously, your life simply *can't* remain the same.

Seek God and dream big. Refuse to fear failure. It's time to venture out. To trust. To dare. To believe. Your life won't always feel safe. And it will take faith. But without faith, it's impossible to please God.

What are you waiting for?

Close the book.

Open your heart.

Cry out to God.

Pray.

DISCUSSION QUESTIONS

INTRODUCTION

1. On a scale of 1–10 (with one representing pathetically lame and ten representing passionately faith-fueled), what would you rank your prayer life last week and why?
2. How has praying been easy for you? When have you found praying to be more of a challenge? Why?
3. When you were growing up, was prayer a part of your life? If so, describe what part it played.
4. Is there a dangerous prayer that you know you should be praying but are afraid to pray? Talk about it openly.
5. If God helped you grow in one area of your prayer life, what do you think it would be and why? Describe.

PART 1: SEARCH ME

1. A lot of people will say or believe that they have a "good heart." But we learned in this chapter that the heart is deceitful (Jer. 17:9). Can you think of a time that your heart led you to do something that you shouldn't have done? Did you rationalize something? How did your heart lead you astray?

2. When David was in a dark place, he prayed the dangerous prayer, "Search me, God" (Ps. 139:23). Have you ever asked God to search you? If not, why not? If you have, what did he show you?

3. David asked God to reveal his "anxious thoughts" (see Ps. 139:23). What concerns or burdens are making you anxious? Is something weighing on you or keeping you awake at night?

4. We also watched as David bravely asked God to show him if there was anything offensive in him (see Ps. 139:24). Have you ever asked God to show you your sinfulness? Did he ever reveal something in you that he wanted to cleanse or change? If so, describe what happened.

5. David prayed the dangerous prayer inviting God to "search him"—to lead him and direct his steps. Has God ever prompted you, spoken to you, or nudged you to do something after you prayed? Or maybe he showed you something through a sermon, or in a song, or from a friend. Talk about a time when you know that God was leading you.

PART 2: BREAK ME

1. Scripture shows again and again how hard times can make us stronger and bring us closer to God. Describe a time when you experienced something difficult and yet recognized God's goodness was with you in the trial.

2. In chapter 2, we looked at 1 Corinthians 11:24, which says, "When [Jesus] had given thanks, he broke [the bread] and said, 'This is my body, which is for you; do this in remembrance of me.'" If you have been around church, you may have experienced Communion or the Lord's Supper. What does this sacrament mean to you? Describe.

3. Some might say that inviting God to "break them" is the most scary of the three dangerous prayers. If you had the courage to ask God to break you, what are you afraid he might do? If your fears actually came to pass, how do you think God would show himself to you?

4. Who do you know that has experienced deep pain and is stronger spiritually on the other side of the brokenness? How is God using them now?

5. If you took time to invite God to break you, what do you think he'd want to remove from your life first? Would he break you of selfishness? Of pride? Of self-sufficiency? Or of something else? Talk about it and explain why.

PART 3: SEND ME

1. In this chapter, we looked at the prayer of Isaiah when he said, "Here I am. Send me" (Isa. 6:8 NLT). I am sometimes nervous to pray this prayer because of fear of where God might send me or what he'll ask me to do. Can you relate?

2. Are you surrendered—completely available—to God right now? Are you doing everything he is leading you to do? Or are you guarded? Resisting? Please discuss openly. Encourage each other toward deeper connection with God.

3. In the sixth chapter of Isaiah, the prophet experienced the presence of God in a way he never had before. When you think of experiencing God's presence, what comes to mind? Have you ever sensed that God was with you? Is it a rare experience? Or is it often? How or when do you experience God best?

4. In this chapter, we looked at the principle, "what you feed grows and what you starve dies." Can you describe a time when feeding your spirit with truth helped you grow? How did God give you the ability to overcome doing something wrong and grow closer to him? Describe.

5. Any act of faith can help you grow closer to God. Talk about the last thing that you did that required faith in God on your part. What happened? What did you learn? Are you ready to let God "send you" no matter where it leads?

CONCLUSION

1. If God said yes to every prayer you prayed in the last week, what would be different in this world today? Be specific.

2. In the conclusion we looked at a prayer attributed to Sir Francis Drake. He asked God to "disturb him." How has God disturbed you as a result of reading this book? What is God showing you about your prayer life? About your faith?

3. Of the three prayers—*search me*, *break me*, and *send me*—which one is the most difficult for you to pray and why?

4. Of the three prayers—*search me*, *break me*, and *send me*—which one are you most ready to pray and why?

5. We looked at three dangerous prayers. If you think about it, I'm sure there are dozens of others that come to mind. If you added a fourth dangerous prayer, what would it be and why?

PRAY A DANGEROUS PRAYER TODAY

The Bible is full of dangerous prayers. King David, the apostle Paul, and even Jesus all prayed their own versions of dangerous prayers. As we learned in the introduction to this book, they prayed honest prayers—desperate, fiery, gutsy, real prayers.

In their own words they said *search me, break me, and send me.*

The dangerous prayers of the Bible can be the fuel for your dangerous prayers today. Isaiah's voice might help you find yours. Esther's words might help you discover fresh words for yourself.

What follows is a brief list of the dangerous prayers found in the Bible. If you are having trouble praying, then start with these. Read through them and adapt them to fit your situation. Allow the words of the followers of God who have gone before you to inspire you, and to help you find words of your own.

Getting Started with Prayer

Jesus taught his disciples to pray by providing them with an example, a passage now widely called the Lord's Prayer. You can pray the exact words of these verses as your own. Meditate on them. Memorize them. You'll probably recognize much of this prayer already.

> "This, then, is how you should pray: 'Our Father in heaven, hallowed be your name, your kingdom come, your will be done, on earth as it is in heaven. Give us today our daily bread. And forgive us our debts, as we also have forgiven our debtors. And lead us not into temptation, but deliver us from the evil one.'"
>
> —MATTHEW 6:9–13

Something great about this prayer is that it doesn't have an "amen" ending. It feels open ended. You can pray these words, then share with God a sentence or two from your heart before saying amen.

"Search Me" Prayers

Psalm 139 is an open and honest prayer before God about how nothing is hidden from him. Open your heart to God. Pray it as your own.

You have searched me, LORD, and you know me. You know when I sit and when I rise; you perceive my thoughts from afar. You discern my going out and my lying down; you are familiar with all my ways. Before a word is on my tongue you, LORD, know it completely. You hem me in behind and before, and you lay your hand upon me. Such knowledge is too wonderful for me, too lofty for me to attain.

Search me, God, and know my heart; test me and know my anxious thoughts. See if there is any offensive way in me, and lead me in the way everlasting.

—PSALM 139:1–6, 23–24

Pray this short psalm from David that screams "search me!" during a time of stress and danger.

How long, LORD? Will you forget me forever? How long will you hide your face from me? How long must I wrestle with my thoughts and day after day have sorrow in my heart? How long will my enemy triumph over me?

Look on me and answer, LORD my God. Give light to my eyes, or I will sleep in death, and my enemy will say, "I have overcome him," and my foes will rejoice when I fall.

But I trust in your unfailing love; my heart rejoices in your salvation. I will sing the LORD's praise, for he has been good to me.

—PSALM 13

"Break Me" Prayers

Jesus set *the* example for us of what it means to pray "break me."

When [Jesus] had given thanks, he broke [the bread] and said, "This is my body, which is for you; do this in remembrance of me."

—1 CORINTHIANS 11:24, PRAYED
DURING THE LAST SUPPER

"Father, if you are willing, take this cup from me; yet not my will, but yours be done."

—LUKE 22:42, PRAYED ON THE
NIGHT JESUS WAS ARRESTED

"Send Me" Prayers

Pray the prophet Isaiah's dangerous, vulnerable words to God:

Then I heard the voice of the Lord saying, "Whom shall I send? And who will go for us?" And I said, "Here am I. Send me!"

—ISAIAH 6:8

Pray like Esther, a young woman who was willing to put her own life on the line in order to protect God's people:

"Go, gather together all the Jews who are in Susa, and fast for me. Do not eat or drink for three days, night or day. I and my attendants will fast as you do. When this is done, I will go to the king, even though it is against the law. And if I perish, I perish."

—ESTHER 4:16

Read and pray all of Psalm 40 if you can. This is an incredible chapter in the Bible. Pray out loud the verses that connect with your circumstances. David said, "Send me!"

I proclaim your saving acts in the great assembly; I do not seal my lips, LORD, as you know. I do not hide your righteousness in my heart; I speak of your faithfulness and your saving help. I do not conceal your love and your faithfulness from the great assembly.

—PSALM 40:9–10

Confession Prayers

Psalm 32 is a classic prayer of confession. When we don't confess our sins, it's like our "bones waste away." But God loves you with an "unfailing love." If there is sin in your life that you haven't confessed to God, pray the words of this psalm. Confess. No matter what you've done, you can believe that he "surrounds the one who trusts him."

Blessed is the one whose transgressions are forgiven, whose sins are covered. Blessed is the one whose sin the LORD does not count against them and in whose spirit is no deceit.

When I kept silent, my bones wasted away through my groaning all day long. For day and night your hand was heavy on me; my strength was sapped as in the heat of summer.

Then I acknowledged my sin to you and did not cover up my iniquity. I said, "I will confess my transgressions to the LORD." And you forgave the guilt of my sin.

Therefore let all the faithful pray to you while you may be found; surely the rising of the mighty waters will not reach them. You are my hiding place; you will protect me from trouble and surround me with songs of deliverance.

I will instruct you and teach you in the way you should go; I will counsel you with my loving eye on you. Do not be like the horse or the mule, which have no understanding but must be controlled by bit and bridle or they will not come to you. Many are the woes of the wicked, but the LORD's unfailing love surrounds the one who trusts in him.

Rejoice in the LORD and be glad, you righteous; sing, all you who are upright in heart!

—PSALM 32

I cry aloud to the LORD; I lift up my voice to the LORD for mercy. I pour out before him my complaint; before him I tell my trouble.

When my spirit grows faint within me, it is you who watch over my way. In the path where I walk people have hidden a snare for me. Look and see, there is no one at my right hand; no one is concerned for me. I have no refuge; no one cares for my life.

I cry to you, LORD; I say, "You are my refuge, my portion in the land of the living."

Listen to my cry, for I am in desperate need; rescue me from those who pursue me, for they are too strong for me. Set me free from my prison, that I may praise your name. Then the righteous will gather about me because of your goodness to me.

—PSALM 142

Some of King David's worst moments are recorded in 2 Samuel 11 and 12. His sins took the lives of others and broke one family apart. Psalm 51 records his confession after those events. No matter what you've done, use the words of this psalm and go to God in prayer.

Have mercy on me, O God, according to your unfailing love; according to your great compassion blot out my transgressions. Wash away all my iniquity and cleanse me from my sin.

For I know my transgressions, and my sin is always before me. Against you, you only, have I sinned and done what is evil in your sight; so you are right in your verdict and justified when you judge. Surely I was sinful at birth, sinful from the time my mother conceived me. Yet you desired faithfulness even in the womb; you taught me wisdom in that secret place.

Cleanse me with hyssop, and I will be clean; wash me, and I will be whiter than snow. Let me hear joy and gladness; let the bones you have crushed rejoice. Hide your face from my sins and blot out all my iniquity.

Create in me a pure heart, O God, and renew a steadfast spirit within me. Do not cast me from your presence or take your Holy Spirit from me. Restore to me the joy of your salvation and grant me a willing spirit, to sustain me.

—PSALM 51:1–12

When Life Is Unbearable

This psalm will give words to your pain and your waiting and remind you of God's incredible power and love.

Hear my prayer, LORD; let my cry for help come to you. Do not hide your face from me when I am in distress. Turn your ear to me; when I call, answer me quickly.

For my days vanish like smoke; my bones burn like glowing embers. My heart is blighted and withered like grass; I forget to eat my food. In my distress I groan aloud and am reduced to skin and bones. I am like a desert owl, like an owl among the ruins. I lie awake; I have become like a bird alone on a roof. All day long my enemies taunt me; those who rail against me use my name as a curse. For I eat ashes as my food and mingle my drink with tears because of your great wrath, for you have taken me up and thrown me aside. My days are like the evening shadow; I wither away like grass.

—PSALM 102:1–11

Did you know that Jesus also prayed with the words of Scripture? He prayed parts of the Psalms as he hung on the cross. When life is unbearable, pray as Jesus prayed: voice your honest feelings before God, then commit your spirit—your life, your heart, your worries—to him.

About three in the afternoon Jesus cried out in a loud voice, "*Eli, Eli, lema sabachthani?*" (which means "My God, my God, why have you forsaken me?").

—MATTHEW 27:46

Jesus called out with a loud voice, "Father, into your hands I commit my spirit." When he had said this, he breathed his last.

—LUKE 23:46

Prayers for Healing

When you or someone you know is sick or struggling physically, you can cry out to God and ask for healing. Consider praying the words of this psalm.

> Have mercy on me, LORD, for I am faint; heal me, LORD, for my bones are in agony. My soul is in deep anguish. How long, LORD, how long?
>
> Turn, LORD, and deliver me; save me because of your unfailing love. Among the dead no one proclaims your name. Who praises you from the grave?
>
> I am worn out from my groaning.
>
> All night long I flood my bed with weeping and drench my couch with tears. My eyes grow weak with sorrow; they fail because of all my foes.
>
> Away from me, all you who do evil, for the LORD has heard my weeping. The LORD has heard my cry for mercy; the LORD accepts my prayer.
>
> —PSALM 6:2–9

Paul knew what it was like to suffer physically. The Bible records that he was flogged, stoned, shipwrecked, and threatened on multiple occasions. Pray his words and find renewal in God's Holy Spirit.

May the God of hope fill you with all joy and peace as you trust in him, so that you may overflow with hope by the power of the Holy Spirit.

—ROMANS 15:13

Prayers of Praise

Pray these words in the sunshine. Pray them in a storm. Pray them on bad days and good days. Pray them to remember that "you are his" no matter what your days are like.

Shout for joy to the LORD, all the earth. Worship the LORD with gladness; come before him with joyful songs. Know that the LORD is God. It is he who made us, and we are his; we are his people, the sheep of his pasture.

Enter his gates with thanksgiving and his courts with praise; give thanks to him and praise his name. For the LORD is good and his love endures forever; his faithfulness continues through all generations.

—PSALM 100

Sometimes the circumstances of life are so ugly that we must look outside ourselves in order to praise God. Pray the words of this psalm to be drawn into the natural world and back into God's Word.

The heavens declare the glory of God; the skies proclaim the work of his hands. Day after day they pour forth speech; night after night they reveal knowledge. They have no speech, they use no words; no sound is heard from them. Yet their voice goes out into all the earth, their words to the ends of the world. In the heavens God has pitched a tent for the sun. It is like a bridegroom coming out of his chamber, like a champion rejoicing to run his course. It rises at one end of the heavens and makes its circuit to the other; nothing is deprived of its warmth.

The law of the LORD is perfect, refreshing the soul. The statutes of the LORD are trustworthy, making wise the simple. The precepts of the LORD are right, giving joy to the heart. The commands of the LORD are radiant, giving light to the eyes. The fear of the LORD is pure, enduring forever. The decrees of the LORD are firm, and all of them are righteous.

They are more precious than gold, than much pure gold; they are sweeter than honey, than honey from the honeycomb. By them your servant is warned; in keeping them there is great reward. But who can discern their own errors? Forgive my hidden faults. Keep your servant also from willful sins; may they not rule over me. Then I will be blameless, innocent of great transgression.

May these words of my mouth and this meditation of my heart be pleasing in your sight, LORD, my Rock and my Redeemer.

—PSALM 19

Prayer for Unity

Did you know that Jesus prayed for you? John 17 records a prayer of Jesus that includes "all who will believe in me." It's a prayer for unity of spirit and purpose.

> "My prayer is not for them alone. I pray also for those who will believe in me through their message, that all of them may be one, Father, just as you are in me and I am in you. May they also be in us so that the world may believe that you have sent me. I have given them the glory that you gave me, that they may be one as we are one—I in them and you in me—so that they may be brought to complete unity. Then the world will know that you sent me and have loved them even as you have loved me."
>
> —JOHN 17:20–23

Purposeful Prayers

When Paul prays, he prays on purpose. Notice in his prayers how often he uses or implies the words "so that."

> For this reason I kneel before the Father, from whom every family in heaven and on earth derives its name. I pray that out of his glorious riches he may strengthen you with

power through his Spirit in your inner being, so that Christ may dwell in your hearts through faith. And I pray that you, being rooted and established in love, may have power, together with all the Lord's holy people, to grasp how wide and long and high and deep is the love of Christ, and to know this love that surpasses knowledge—that you may be filled to the measure of all the fullness of God.

Now to him who is able to do immeasurably more than all we ask or imagine, according to his power that is at work within us, to him be glory in the church and in Christ Jesus throughout all generations, for ever and ever! Amen.

—EPHESIANS 3:14–21

For this reason, since the day we heard about you, we have not stopped praying for you. We continually ask God to fill you with the knowledge of his will through all the wisdom and understanding that the Spirit gives, so that you may live a life worthy of the Lord and please him in every way: bearing fruit in every good work, growing in the knowledge of God, being strengthened with all power according to his glorious might so that you may have great endurance and patience, and giving joyful thanks to the Father, who has qualified you to share in the inheritance of his holy people in the kingdom of light.

—COLOSSIANS 1:9–12

And this is my prayer: that your love may abound
more and more in knowledge and depth of insight, so that
you may be able to discern what is best and may be pure
and blameless for the day of Christ, filled with the fruit of
righteousness that comes through Jesus Christ—to the glory
and praise of God.

—PHILIPPIANS 1:9–11

Prayers of Blessing

Our God is a kind, gracious, and loving heavenly Father who
delights in blessing his children. As you spend time talking to
God, you can ask him to bless you and those you love.

"The LORD bless you and keep you; the LORD make his
face shine on you and be gracious to you; the LORD turn his
face toward you and give you peace."

—NUMBERS 6:24–26

Jabez cried out to the God of Israel, "Oh, that you would
bless me and enlarge my territory! Let your hand be with
me, and keep me from harm so that I will be free from pain."
And God granted his request.

—1 CHRONICLES 4:10

Prayers of Guidance

Sometimes knowing the next best step to take is incredibly challenging. Pray these words of David when you aren't sure what God would have you do.

In you, LORD my God, I put my trust.

I trust in you; do not let me be put to shame, nor let my enemies triumph over me....

Show me your ways, LORD, teach me your paths. Guide me in your truth and teach me, for you are God my Savior, and my hope is in you all day long. Remember, LORD, your great mercy and love, for they are from of old.

—PSALM 25:1–2, 4–6

"If you are pleased with me, teach me your ways so I may know you and continue to find favor with you."

—EXODUS 33:13

Prayer for Boldness

Though we may truly love God, sometimes we hesitate to share our faith with others. We don't want to offend them or fear that we don't know enough to answer all of their spiritual questions. When we feel timid or afraid, we can ask God to give us the boldness to share with others.

> "Now, Lord, consider their threats and enable your servants to speak your word with great boldness. Stretch out your hand to heal and perform signs and wonders through the name of your holy servant Jesus."
>
> —ACTS 4:29–30

Prayer for Salvation and Help

If you know the story of Jonah at all, then you know this prayer speaks volumes. Praise God today with these words. He has saved you. Salvation comes from the Lord! Shout it from the rooftops.

> "In my distress I called to the LORD, and he answered me. From deep in the realm of the dead I called for help, and you listened to my cry. You hurled me into the depths, into the very heart of the seas, and the currents swirled about me; all your waves and breakers swept over me. I said, 'I have been banished from your sight; yet I will look again toward your holy temple.' The engulfing waters threatened me, the deep surrounded me; seaweed was wrapped around my head. To the roots of the mountains I sank down; the

earth beneath barred me in forever. But you, LORD my God, brought my life up from the pit.

"When my life was ebbing away, I remembered you, LORD, and my prayer rose to you, to your holy temple.

"Those who cling to worthless idols turn away from God's love for them. But I, with shouts of grateful praise, will sacrifice to you. What I have vowed I will make good. I will say, 'Salvation comes from the LORD.'"

—JONAH 2:2–9

ACKNOWLEDGMENTS

Thank you to all my friends who offered support, encouragement, and assistance with this book.

I'm especially thankful for:

Dudley Delffs: You are a blast to work with. (And yes, I just ended a sentence with a preposition to annoy you.) I have loved working with you on every book. Your friendship is a gift.

David Morris, Brandon Henderson, Tom Dean, Andy Rogers, Brian Phipps, Lori Vanden Bosch, and the whole team at Zondervan: I love your commitment to excellence and Christ-centered publishing.

Tom Winters: Thanks for believing in me and pushing for the best.

Tanner Blom, Lori Meeks, Adrianne Manning, and Stephanie Pok: You are the office dream team. Thank you for all you do to make my life better and our church family stronger.

Amy: You are my favorite prayer warrior. I'm looking forward to growing old with you (which is happening way faster than either of us expected).

Hope in the Dark
Believing God Is Good When Life Is Not

In the midst of great pain, we may wonder if God really cares about us. Pastor Craig Groeschel invites us to wrestle with our questions and doubts while honoring our faith and asking God to heal our unbelief. Rediscover faith in the character, power, and presence of God.

The Christian Atheist
Believing in God but Living as If He Doesn't Exist

Join bestselling author and pastor, Craig Groeschel as he unpacks his personal walk toward an authentic God-honoring life. Groeschel's frank and raw conversation about our Christian Atheist tendencies and habits is a convicting and life-changing read.

Liking Jesus
Intimacy and Contentment in a Selfie-Centered World

Keep your eyes fixed on Christ instead of glued to a screen. Craig Groeschel teaches how to break unmanageable digital dependency and regain control of your life. *Liking Jesus* is a guide to bringing a balance of spiritual depth and human engagement back to your life.

Soul Detox
Clean Living in a Contaminated World

Without even knowing it, people willingly inhale second-hand cultural toxins poisoning their relationship with God and stunting their spiritual growth. *Soul Detox* examines the toxins that assault us daily, including toxic influences, toxic emotions, and toxic behaviors, and offers spiritual intervention with ways to remain focused on God's holy standards.

Fight
Winning the Battles That Matter Most

Fight helps uncover your true identity—a powerful man with a warrior's heart. With God's help, you'll find the strength to fight battles you know must be won: the ones that determine the state of your heart, quality of your marriage, and spiritual health of those you love most.

Divine Direction
Seven Decisions That Will Change Your Life

In this inspiring guidebook, bestselling author Craig Groeschel illustrates how the choices you make connect you to God and can lead you to a life you've only imagined. The achievable, disciplined, and simple steps in *Divine Direction* can take your life to wonderful and unexpected places only God could've planned.

Daily Power
365 Days of Fuel for Your Soul

Bestselling author Craig Groeschel's daily devotional will help you develop a consistent, daily pursuit of Jesus. In 365 brief devotions, Craig shares insights from his life that you can apply to almost every area of your own. *Daily Power* is here to help you grow and become strong every day of the year.

It Book with DVD
How Churches and Leaders Can Get It and Keep It

It. The life-changing, powerful force that draws people to you. What is *It* and how can you and your ministry get—and keep—*It*? Combining raw honesty with off-the-wall humor, this book explains how any believer can find *It*, get *It* back, and guard *It*.

Expand your leadership potential.

CRAIG GROESCHEL
LEADERSHIP PODCAST

Subscribe to the **Craig Groeschel Leadership Podcast**
on iTunes and Google Play.

Visit **www.life.church/leadershippodcast** to find
episode notes, application guides, and more.

 MUSIC   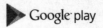 Google play

Hundreds of millions of people are using the *YouVersion Bible App* to make God's Word a part of their daily lives.

Download the free app and access your bookmarks, notes, and reading plans from anywhere. Enjoy hundreds of versions, including audio, all on your mobile device.

Find practical leadership insights,
discover more books from Craig, and
see where Craig will be speaking next.

craiggroeschel.com.